Verses From London

Edited by Aimée Vanstone

 Young**Writers**

First published in Great Britain in 2008 by:
Young Writers
Remus House
Coltsfoot Drive
Peterborough
PE2 9JX
Telephone: 01733 890066
Website: www.youngwriters.co.uk

SB ISBN 978-1 84431 654 0

Foreword

Young Writers was established in 1991 and has been passionately devoted to the promotion of reading and writing in children and young adults ever since. The quest continues today. Young Writers remains as committed to the nurturing of poetic and literary talent as ever.

This year's Young Writers competition has proven as vibrant and dynamic as ever and we are delighted to present a showcase of the best poetry from across the UK and in some cases overseas. Each poem has been selected from a wealth of *Little Laureates 2008* entries before ultimately being published in this, our seventeenth primary school poetry series.

Once again, we have been supremely impressed by the overall quality of the entries we have received. The imagination, energy and creativity which has gone into each young writer's entry made choosing the poems a challenging and often difficult but ultimately hugely rewarding task - the general high standard of the work submitted ensured this opportunity to bring their poetry to a larger appreciative audience.

We sincerely hope you are pleased with this final collection and that you will enjoy *Little Laureates 2008 Verses From London* for many years to come.

Contents

Ravenscourt Park Preparatory School

Hannah Darling (11)	54
Joe Grieve (10)	54
Harry Coke (10)	55
Toby Clyde (10)	55
Oscar Mayhew (11)	56
Anna Kerr (11)	56
Amelia Gosztony (11)	57
Oscar Jenkyn-Jones (10)	57
Elsa Darlington (10)	58
Adam Plavsic (11)	59
Hugo French (9)	60
Stanley Love (11)	60
Anna Burnett (10)	61
Ella Burdett (10)	61
Gregor Fuller (10)	62
Eliza Baring (9)	62
Amelia Lloyd (10)	63
Maisie Cowell (9)	63
Harry Mayes (11)	64
Luca Cericola (10)	65
Alexander Fassone (10)	65
Alex Pigott (9)	66
Lizzie Bramley (9)	66
Emma Olrik (9)	67
Imogen Cunningham (10)	67
Matthew Piercy (9)	68
Alexander Rugman (9)	68
Charlotte Stapleton (9)	69
Joe Lister (8)	69
Finn Brown (9)	70
Ella Lindsay (9)	71
Thomas Polyblank (10)	72
Hope Coke (9)	72
Freddie Foulkes (8)	73

St Ann's CE Primary School, Tottenham

Ellen Smith (9)	73

St Benedict's Junior School, Ealing

Adeyemi Adeola (9)	74

Bogdan de Berg (10)   74
Tristan Jenkin-Gomez (8)   75
Oliver Buchanan (9)   75
Olivia Smith (9)   76
Sam Scott (10)   77
Rory Hobson (11)   78
Theodore Hyams (7)   79
Francesca O'Neill (9)   80
Charlie Sanderson (10)   80
Liam Carty-Howe (8)   81
Toby McDonald (8)   81
Evie Gracie-Barnes (10)   82
Joshua Wood (10)   82
Stelios Souvaliotis (11)   83
Francis Curran (10)   83
Oliver Clark (11)   84
Christy Creighton (11)   84
Guy McDonald (9)   85
Samuel Jury (9)   85
Thomas Zussman (7)   86
Daniel Michael (9)   86
Tiernan Sheehan (11)   87
Chay Siu (10)   87
Lucy Bartle (10)   88
James Porter (10)   88
George Charlesworth (7)   89
William Davies (8)   89
Thomas Sanders (9)   90
Sean Anthony (8)   90
Ellie Scott (9)   91
Rachel de Cintra (8)   91
George Johnson (9)   92
Alex Mitchell-Bruguera (9)   92
Henry Goode (10)   93
William Poyntz (9)   93
Sam Loveless (10)   94
Benedict Chippendale (9)   94

St Charles RC Primary School, London

Patricia Tran (9)   95
Chioma Okeke-Aru (8)   95

Dean-Emmanuelly Kamna (11)   96
Jowayne James (8)   96
Rianna Hinds (9)   96
Simone Almario (10)   97

St James Independent School, London
Rosie Lim (10)   97
Aylin Ozbicer (10)   97
Amy Douglas-Morris (10)   98
Ava Halvai (11)   98
Zoe Hewitt (10)   99
Imogen Willis (11)   99
Tara Saheli Vyas (10)   100
Ashleigh John (11)   100
Jessica Cselko (11)   101
Amanda Ruth Waters (11)   101
Liberty Ann Pearl (11)   102
Francesca Kynan-Holmes (11)   102
Tatyana Rutherston (10)   103
Aarti Nayak (10)   103
Olivia Kelly (10)   104
Lara Dingemans (10)   105
Elva Vuskovic Enninful (11)   105
Ella Wills (10)   106
Zoë MacLellan (11)   106
Elizabeth Witkowski (10)   107
Nenaz Babaee (11)   107

St John Evangelist RC Primary School, London
Benedict Parker (9)   108
Andrew George Whiting (8)   108
Lauren Jade Healy (9)   109
Louis Nathan Oliva (8)   109
Scarlett Malynn (7)   110
Harvey Grace (9)   110
Kayleigh Harold (7)   111
Megan Wills (9)   111
Alfie Dundon (8)   111
Henry Jay White (8)   112
Rachel Burgess (8)   112
Tilly Townsend (8)   112

Caighlyn Christina Magee-Biggs (8)   113
Andres Florez (8)   113
Andrew Osborne (9)   113
Connor Gannon (8)   114

St Mary's RC Primary School, Chiswick
Maeve Johnson (8)   114
Emer Walsh (8)   114
William Edward Walsh (9)   115
Ryan Munasinghe (8)   115
Millie Atherton (8)   116
Ciara Clarke (8)   116
Thomas Rooney (9)   117
Charlotte Purcell (9)   117
Georgina Boyle (9)   118
Isobel Brophy (9)   118
Peter Martin-Collar (9)   118
Sarah Duns (9)   119
Chantal O'Toole (9)   119
Emily Badra (8)   119
Luca James Lota (8)   120
Eleanor Jones (9)   120
Conor Raymie Sugden (9)   120
Samantha Fuller (8)   121
Luca Dilieto (8)   121
Oliver James Israel (9)   121
Molly George (8)   122
John James Edward Dobbs (9)   122
Lydia Hopgood (8)   122
Eoin Murphy (9)   123
Sean Flynn (9)   123

St Pauls & All Hallows CE Junior School, Tottenham
Danielle Fearon (9)   124
Betty Oppong-Kusi (10)   125
Ibukun Omibiyi (10)   126
Rhoda Akaka (11)   127
Shakira Dyer (10)   128

St Paul's RC Primary School, Wood Green

St Stephen's CE Primary School, Shepherds Bush

Sir Thomas Abney School

The Poems

Love - Good Or Bad?

Love is an extremely popular emotion, Its colour is mauve like the beautiful dawn in summer.
It sounds like an old, eerie violin in a posh restaurant full of chattering and singing.
It smells like a gorgeous cake mixture, ready for a wedding.

When I think of love it reminds me of champagne and confetti, and a rose, reaching out as though it were to kiss me, though it's neither a good or a bad thing, as it can lead to envy, but if successful, is the best feeling ever.

When you feel love, you always know, it creeps up on you like a forget-me-not in a sweet-smelling garden and fizzles up inside you like fireworks, turning your stomach into a choppy sea.
It looks like the feathery, colourful velvet on a baby hummingbird, waiting calmly for its mother to return with food.
Romance tastes so similar to Quality Street chocolates, you wouldn't be able to tell the difference apart from love, just tasting like a posh meal or honey.

Love can be very dangerous, so be careful how you use it, for if you use it incorrectly, you will regret it!

Ellie Louise Grant (11)
All Saints CE Primary School

Anger

Anger is red like the Devil,
And it sounds like blood dripping from a blade.
It looks like an active volcano,
It feels like an earthquake shaking your heart away.

It reminds me of the fire of London,
Destroying everything in its path.

Charlie Batten (11) & Nicholas Zertalis (10)
All Saints CE Primary School

Jealousy

Jealousy is green like a bush of stinging nettles.
It sounds like a deep organ playing.
It looks like a shadow and you all can see are the green eyes in
the darkness.

It smells like a steaming gooey swamp.
It tastes like a sour green lemon.
It feels like something is controlling my brain and I can't get it out.
It reminds me of a green-eyed monster on my shoulder telling me
what to do.

Lizzie Putt (11), Eden Higgins & Clara Lenzi (10)
All Saints CE Primary School

Happiness

Happiness is yellow like the shining, shimmering sun.
In the distance I hear laughter and joy from every girl and boy.
It looks like Heaven at last, there's luscious green grass,
Birds flying high up in the blue sky.
It feels like home at last with the warmth of the sun shining
upon us so vast.
It tastes like melting chocolate with whipped cream on the side.
It reminds us of dolphins swimming across the ocean.

Sophie Symeou & Jodi Coleman (10)
All Saints CE Primary School

Love

Love is red like a big bouquet of red roses freshly picked.
Love sounds like a hummingbird in the morning.
Love looks like a garden in summer with every flower open.
Love feels like you have been trapped all your life but now you are free.
Love smells like fresh bread, just out of the stove.
Love tastes like satisfaction.

Georgia Spencer (10)
All Saints CE Primary School

Happiness

Happiness is yellow like a swirling daffodil.
It sounds like bubbles in a bubbling stream.
It looks like a golden glowing sky.
It feels like your desires are coming true.
It smells like a garden full of flowers and happiness.
It tastes like chocolate from a chocolate fountain.

Happiness reminds you of the sun and people getting along.

Jasmine Mohammad & Aidan Poles (10)
All Saints CE Primary School

Shock

Shock is dark blue like a stormy sea.
It sounds like a heartbeat stopping instantly.
It looks like everything is frozen in time.
It feels like a zooming car hitting you at its highest speed.
It smells like choking black smoke.
It tastes like cold, weary air.
It reminds me of someone jumping out on me on a dark night!

Grace Corkill (10) & Amber Salomone (11)
All Saints CE Primary School

Love

Love is pink like blossoms blooming in springtime.
It tastes like sweet honey, fresh from the beehives.
It looks like a beautiful big heart, waiting to engulf the world with love.
Love smells like fresh candy, straight from the moulds.
It feels like soft silk, fresh from the loom.
Love sounds like soft, sweet birds whistling to the wind.
It reminds me of a never-ending dream filled with joy and happiness.

That's what love is!

Jeronee Jennycloss & Mia Fearon (11)
All Saints CE Primary School

Happiness

Happiness is like a huge yellow sunflower.
It sounds like a beautiful bird whistling day and night.
It looks like a spring garden in the morning,
covered with a blanket of dew over the grass.
It feels like a new life arriving every day.
It smells like a pink bud growing into a wonderful rose.
It tastes like life has been freshly made out of the oven,
just like French bread.
It reminds me of waking up in the morning and hearing nature
calling out happiness.

Chloe Celine Fisher (11)
All Saints CE Primary School

Happiness

Happiness is yellow like the sunrise in the early morning.
It sounds like children laughing and playing.
It looks so beautiful like a bright red rose.
It makes you so relaxed.
It smells of the beautiful green grass.
Happiness tastes of the fresh mid-air.
It reminds me of a wonderful holiday at the beach.

Sheel Kothari (11)
All Saints CE Primary School

Anger

Anger sounds like the drum roll
Anger is red like an exploding volcano,
Anger smells like burning flesh,
Anger feels like the Devil's brother,
Anger tastes like leftover ashes.

Tamim Miah (10)
All Saints CE Primary School

Fear

A black river of fear flows through the land
Sounds like the beating and drumming of a band
The ghastly stench engulfs the air
Brings back memories of a fierce black bear
Takes the form of fighting, nightmares and loss
Brings the anxiousness of being fired by your boss
Tastes bitter, sweet, sour, disgusting and bad
Don't go near *fear*, for you'll lose all you had . . .

Hussein Mansour, Theodore Buttigieg (10)
& Rubin Khojasteh (11)
All Saints CE Primary School

Anger

Anger sounds like a drum beating faster and faster.
Anger is the colour red like the Devil.
Anger is the Devil's rage.
Anger is the rampage of the elephants.
Anger is the taste of sour lemons.
Anger smells like burning ash.

Anthony Zorbis (10)
All Saints CE Primary School

Fear

Fear is grey like ashes of a fire.
It smells like rotting rubbish.
It looks like a dark rain cloud.
It sounds like a parade of soldiers in my head.
And it feels like a hand gripping my shoulder in a dark alleyway.
It reminds me of a horrible nightmare.

Daniel Maynard (10)
All Saints CE Primary School

Anger's Here

Anger is red like an exploding volcano
It's things like that that make me shout, 'No!'

Anger sounds like a broken violin
And we all know that's a sin

Anger looks like a dead rabbit
And I know who killed it. Sorry, it's just my habit

Anger smells like rotten food
I know I didn't buy that Robin Hood

Anger reminds me of when I lost my game
I killed every rabbit that looks the same!

Peter Jacquaye (10)
All Saints CE Primary School

Love Is . . .

Love is a pink rose opening into the air,
Love sounds like the kissing of two sweet lips,
Love spills a tear of happiness and joy,
Love is the smell of Heaven above,
Love is the feeling of two bare hands holding,
Love is the taste of honey,
Love is a couple lasting forever.

Joshua Navarajasegaran (11)
All Saints CE Primary School

Anger

Anger is red like a little angry devil cackling and waving
                                        his sharp trident.
It sounds like a snorting, raging bull.
It tastes like a ton of Nando's hot peri-peri sauce!
Anger smells like lots of spices mixed into an anger pie.
It looks like a hissing, fire-breathing dragon about to burn
                                        down a castle.
Anger feels like you're a big balloon and someone's blowing
                                        you up bigger and bigger.
It reminds me of a cheetah growling in frustration because
                                        he didn't catch his prey.

Harry Abraham (8)
Christ Church Primary School

Happiness

Happiness is yellow like the bright shine of the sun,
It sounds like a little girl laughing,
It tastes like the sweet taste of sugar,
Happiness smells like the delightful smell of ice cream,
It looks like a cute smiling face,
It feels like the softness of the golden sand,
It reminds me of lavender.

Flora Sayers (7)
Christ Church Primary School

Happiness

Happiness is cream like white, deep, wavy, cold water,
Happiness sounds like going on a slippery, high slide splashing
                                                    with water,
It tastes like Aero minty hot chocolate with bubbles popping in
                                                    your mouth,
It smells like a rose-smelling perfume,
It looks like a shiny star blasting with glitter coming out of it,
It feels like a freezing hard ice lolly,
It reminds me of a pale white lily.

Parinaz Pedrampour (8)
Christ Church Primary School

Calm

Calmness is peach like my soft skin,
It sounds like a still, floating river, quiet as a mouse creeping
                                    through my cat's territory,
It tastes like mouth-watering mint bubblegum,
Calmness smells like minty tea leaves,
It looks like the peaceful countryside,
It feels like air whizzing around me,
It reminds me of the oracle meditating in Candracar.

Elli Brougham (7)
Christ Church Primary School

Happiness

Happiness is yellow like a happy, smiling, yellow face,
It sounds like a funfair with people laughing and children playing,
It tastes like an ice cream as cool as Antarctica,
Happiness smells like the sweet smell of lavender,
It looks like the sun shining down on the world, a burning hot sun,
It feels like the smooth sand rubbing on my feet,
It reminds me of when I am at a beach or swimming in the sea
                                                    at sunset.

Beth Summers (8)
Christ Church Primary School

Excitement

Excitement is orange like a joyful cheetah running all over Africa.
It sounds like a man shouting because he is happy with his new house.
It tastes like an energy drink made by a famous person from the future.
Excitement smells like a home-made Christmas dinner with
                                    home-grown vegetables.
It looks like a happy, happy kangaroo bouncing as high as the trees.
It sounds like a leaping dog jumping up at a bone its owner has.
It reminds me of a mouse with cheese from the kitchen where
                                    the angry cook is.

Adam Bradley (7)
Christ Church Primary School

Excitement

Excitement is blue like a blue dolphin,
Excitement sounds like me shouting my eyes out!
It tastes like a big piece of white chocolate,
Excitement smells like a big lump of sugar,
It looks like a white rabbit bouncing in the savannah,
Excitement feels like a huge, big, giant, jumping bird in giant land,
It reminds of a kangaroo jumping in Australia.

Raphaelle Killick (7)
Christ Church Primary School

Fury

Fury is red like a burning fire; as red as cherries,
Fury sounds like the roar of a lion guarding his prey,
It tastes like bitter lemons sizzling in my mouth,
Fury smells like a rotten egg cracking and making a disgusting smell,
It looks like an angry tiger's face eating its prey,
Fury feels like the bite of a lion's teeth,
It reminds me of a lion's face.

Caitlin Oldham (8)
Christ Church Primary School

Hunger

Hunger is pale like the pale skin of a child who needs food.
Hunger sounds like my dad's stomach moaning as loud as a
rumbling volcano.
It tastes like dribble in your mouth, like rain falling from the sky.
Hunger smells like an imaginary roast chicken with lots of
gorgeous garlic.
It looks like a hungry drooling mouth.
Hunger feels like you are going to die of starvation.
It reminds me of a homeless child I saw in Brazil searching
for food in a bin.

Stella Jones Macdonald (7)
Christ Church Primary School

Worry

Worry is yellow like a luscious lemon,
It sounds like a tough guy whimpering, and frightening lightning,
It tastes like soft bread,
It smells like burnt toast,
It looks like a grey cloud,
It feels like rough material,
It reminds me of Angus' dog barking and biting like a ferocious lion.

Ed Travers (8)
Christ Church Primary School

Anger

Anger is purple like when your face is angry,
It sounds like a stampede at the beginning of a battle,
It tastes like spicy American pizza burning in your tummy,
It smells like a burning house,
It looks like my mum when she gets angry,
It reminds me of when I fell off a boulder onto another boulder.

Jack Bleakley (7)
Christ Church Primary School

Calm

Calm is peach like a sunrise way up in the dawn
And a cupcake you are eating softly,
It sounds like still bath water with melting soap on it,
It tastes like mint tic-tacs with extra taste,
Calm smells like a tulip growing and new plants as well,
It looks like a magic dolphin with sparkles on it,
Calm feels like soft waves pushing against you,
It reminds me of painting a little girl.

Ela Kaynak (7)
Christ Church Primary School

Anger

Anger is red like red-hot boiling lava,
It sounds like a fierce bull,
It tastes like red-hot chilli pepper,
Anger smells like hot lava,
It looks like an exploding bomb,
Anger feels like scratching your arm,
It reminds me of fighting my brother.

Cormac Bruce (8)
Christ Church Primary School

Mouse

(In memory of my mouse)

Oh my lovely mouse
How I grew so fond of you
But your life flew like a butterfly.

Claudia Baum (10)
Flora Gardens Primary School

Alien

At midnight on one rainy day in November,
(Not really a Monday you'd want to remember),
I woke up in bed, shivering and cold,
I called, 'Cousin Rosie.'
'Shut up,' I was told.

I looked out of my window and screamed in fright,
For there before me, a *very* strange sight!
A flying saucer hovered outside,
Purple and spotty, and rather wide.

I went *plod* down the stairs,
In a rapt sort of gaze,
It was like I was lost
In some sort of maze.

I walked out to the yard,
And under a tree,
I sat on the grass
And a light shone on me.

I rose up in the air
And spun round and round,
I zoomed even higher,
Then fell on some ground.

I stayed for some time
On that uneven floor,
But then I was not on that ground anymore.

I was falling, falling
With increasing speed,
Faster and faster,
Like on a steed.

I hit the ground,
Near a field of llamas,
But I'd turned rather pink,
I was in my pyjamas.

I stared around,
It was really cool,
For I suddenly realised . . .
I was early for school!

Eve Althaus (11)
Flora Gardens Primary School

Dragons

Dragons have lots of shiny scales,
And they leave lots of slimy trails,
They breathe out red-hot fire,
Their dark green ears feel like wire,
If you steal their golden eggs,
They will scrape you with their tall black legs,
Their claws are as sharp as a lion's teeth,
Their tails are as spiky as a pointy, green wreath,
The princess, the dragon had to greet,
To cook some lovely princess meat,
But the handsome prince came galloping by,
And he heard the beautiful princess cry,
He heard the princess hope and hope,
So he tied up the dragon with a thin black rope,
And he heard the princess say, 'You are my hero!'
So he gave the dragon a huge, huge *zero!*
And so off they went to happily play,
They got married that very day!

Minna Althaus (7)
Flora Gardens Primary School

Football Mad!

Football is crazy
When the players fall over the ball they say whoops-a-daisy!
Jerome scores a goal
He's lucky he wasn't born at the North Pole

The crowd cheers '1-0.'
And the next day they look at their bill.
A commentator says, 'What team do you play for?'
'I play for Manchester City.'
'Don't be silly.'
'I am being silly but I will tell you something, my second name
is Billy!'

Manchester City was trying to win the Premiership
And they didn't have any friendship.
Manchester City was first
Could Manchester United do any worse?
Chelsea wanted to say a cuss
But they couldn't because they were last!

Jerome was the top scorer of the season
He's the best player in the world, that was the reason
It has been the best year
And next season Manchester City won't have any fear.

Jerome Richardson (10)
Flora Gardens Primary School

Sea Monster

The sea monster has grisly teeth
And the spikes on its back are as spiky as a wreath!
Its horrible breath lets out a stench
And if you look at it, you will get drenched!
Its slimy scales are as bad as sick
And if you go near it, it will give you a lick!
It only eats child and princess meat
And when it breathes, it lets out a heat!
Its big fat tail squirms in the sea
It's looking for a person and that person is *me!*

Sea monster!

Connie Baum (7)
Flora Gardens Primary School

The Haunted House

The haunted house is spooky and scary
The bats that hide there are black and hairy.

The haunted house has creaky doors
And creepy-crawlies live under the floors.

The haunted house has stairs that creak
And behind every wardrobe is a funny-looking freak.

The haunted house has windows that flap
And the ghost that lives there is a friendly chap!

Grace McWeeney (8)
Larmenier & Sacred Heart RC Primary School

Walking My Dog

The second my dog pounces on me,
I know he is willing to have a walk,
I put on his red beautiful lead,
We walk together down the road,
His golden fur so wonderful, so soft,
At the park we now are,
He runs off so quickly, as quick as a Ferrari sports car,
He runs too far,
I can't see him,
I look and look and look,
He is lost, my playful loving dog, lost!
I'm like a ball of thunder now that I have no dog,
But wait . . . what is that golden moving creature in the distance?
My dog!

Lauryn Pierro (10)
Larmenier & Sacred Heart RC Primary School

The King's Garden

There is a puddle in my back garden
A puddle that never says pardon
'Who are you?' says the puddle
'Don't you know who I am?'
'No.'
'I am the King -
The King of everything!'
'Well, I am the puddle.'
'The puddle?'
'Yes, that's right, the puddle.'
'The same puddle that made me slip?'
'No, the puddle who made you drip!'
'How dare you, foul puddle, I will jump on you!'
'You will get even wetter if you do!'

Amelia Kay (10)
Larmenier & Sacred Heart RC Primary School

Trains

Some trains go very fast
Some trains are always last.
But the train I like best
Is the train that is going to the west.
It takes me directly to Devon
Which is much nearer to Heaven.
At the station Granny meets us
We go by car and not by bus.
Next day we go riding or swimming
My heart with joy is over-brimming.
So I like the train that takes me west
Because Devon really is the best.

Joshua Simpkins (7)
Larmenier & Sacred Heart RC Primary School

Making Snowmen

Rolling the head slowly,
Poking the face crazily,
Bending the arms carefully,
Squeezing the body firmly

Rolling the head quickly,
Poking the face lowly
Bending the arms happily
Squeezing the body angrily.

Rolling the head gently,
Poking the face speedily,
Bending the arms peacefully,
Squeezing the body powerfully.

Theresa Boyo (8)
Larmenier & Sacred Heart RC Primary School

On The Beach

I sit on the beach looking up
I watch the sun go down like a mammal looking for its prey
I see dogs barking like a pack of wolves
And think maybe I will call it a day.

I see the sea going really slow like a snail walking
But suddenly I go cold and wet
Like I've been swimming in Antarctica
Then I open my eyes and see myself on an old bench in the park
I realise I am being licked by dogs!

Joyce Anne Guray (11)
Larmenier & Sacred Heart RC Primary School

Jesus

J esus is the light of the world.
E very day we pray.
S unday is the first day of the week.
U se the bible every day.
S unday is the day we go to church.

Olivia Amadi (8)
Larmenier & Sacred Heart RC Primary School

Turtles

Turtles come from everywhere except Antarctica.
Turtles come in many different colours and sizes,
Swimming around in the sea as an endangered species.

George Whear (7)
Larmenier & Sacred Heart RC Primary School

Kite Flying

I unwind the string and look for the wind
The string pulls tight
I hold on with all my might
Carried by a breeze
Higher and higher above the trees
Fly, fly, fly . . .

Charlie Smith (7)
Larmenier & Sacred Heart RC Primary School

Colours

As purple as blackberry juice
As red as a ruby
As green as an emerald

As orange as an orange
As yellow as the sun
As blue as the sea

As pink as blossom
As brown as chocolate
As black as coal

As grey as an elephant
As gold as a goldfish.

Matt Smith (8)
Little Ealing Primary School

Pet Talk

I like having conversations
With my cat,
About physics and philosophy
And other things like that.
When it comes to talking
My hamster's never shy.
He always talks of cheese
I've never found out why.
Whenever I am cooking
My goldfish likes to chatter,
He waffles about the football
And science stuff like matter.
My beagle's very boring
He's full of useless facts,
The only thing he doesn't know
Is how to use tic-tacs.
You may think pets are peaceful
But I know that you're wrong,
Cos when they start to gossip
They go on and on and on!

Katharine Swindells (11)
Little Ealing Primary School

Colours

Blue as a sky,
Orange as a sweet orange,
Red as dark blood,
Green as grass.

Purple as a felt-tip pen,
Yellow as light thunder,
Brown as rough wood.

Gold as jewellery,
Silver as a ring,
White as a sheet.

Dara Hamo (9)
Little Ealing Primary School

The Highwayman

The highwayman stole across the road,
Like an unpleasant, ugly, odorous toad.
He looked cautiously left and right.
Even the slightest noise would give him a fright!

He saw a valuable in a house,
He crept up like a dirty louse.
Out of his pocket came a skeleton key,
He opened the door with bad, intentional glee.

He took a gold, silver and emerald jewel.
His features twisted, terrible and cruel.
In its place he put a vial of gruel.
This was his sign of a terrible fool!

Nathaniel Rachman (9)
Little Ealing Primary School

The March

R unning, drilling and planning
O nwards we march
M any soldiers just like me
A ttacking Celts, Gauls and Goths along my way
N o discipline whatsoever.

A fierce race indeed
R unning out of line completely
M ice are more civilised
Y ou're surrendering to Rome the almighty!

Jacob Falk (8)
Little Ealing Primary School

Granny Comes For Lunch

When my mum announced
'Granny's coming for lunch,'
I got so annoyed,
'Mum, thanks a bunch!'

Gummy kisses
Afternoon tea
But that's not all
To my granny you see.

Nettle soup
Out of a can
Is a favourite
Of my gran.

Her hour-long lectures
Are such a bore.
Ding-dong! Oh no!
Who's that at the door?

I hope it's postie
On his daily round
But wait,
What's that peculiar sound?

'Hello darling,'
A familiar voice said,
Then I saw my granny
On a *moped!*

Holly Willmott (10)
Little Ealing Primary School

My Cats

C harming cat.
H ungry cat.
A ngry cat.
R arely quiet cat.
L azy cat.
I rritable when asleep cat.
E legance may not be his thing but he's still a loveable cat.

A ngry? Not really.
N ever very sad.
D angerous? Never!

B endy cat.
O utstanding cat.
B rilliant-minded cat.

Emily Bourne (8)
Little Ealing Primary School

Colours

As pink as a pig
As red as a ruby
As orange as an orange

As black as coal
As green as grass
As yellow as the sun

As brown as chocolate
As grey as an elephant
As gold as a goldfish

As silver as moonlight
As purple as an amethyst
As sparkly as a sapphire.

Louis Williams (8)
Little Ealing Primary School

Hallowe'en

It's time to trick or treat,
give me a sweet, or you'll get a beat,
and won't you be daunted
when you see a ghost, because you are haunted . . .

Hey little munchkin, light up that pumpkin!
A ghost fed Ned some poisonous bread, oh no!
Now Ned is dead, there are his bones!
I can hear lots of moans and groans.

It's time to trick or treat,
give me a sweet or you'll get a beat,
and won't you be daunted
when you see a ghost, because you are haunted . . .

I'll give you a scare.
Hey, there's a bear!
There are some ants!
There's a skeleton wearing pants!

It's time to trick or treat,
give me a sweet or you'll get a beat,
and won't you be daunted
when you see a ghost, because you are haunted . . .
Hallowe'en!

Talia Smolar-Fourniol (7)
Little Ealing Primary School

Zoola

I was sitting in the bedroom
But one day,
A rat ran through the hole
And ate my paper,
This reminded me of my dog Zoola.

Zoola would eat anything,
From rulers to cabbage,
Cabbage to paper,
Paper to frogs' eggs,
Frogs' eggs to pizza,
Oh, he would eat anything . . .
Except dog food,
Which was quite weird!

Most dogs would eat dog food,
Because they think it's yummy.
And at the dog test,
My dog tried dog food,
But pushed it to the side,
Which made him last . . .
But he was obedient!

Lauren Latouche-Charles (9)
Little Ealing Primary School

Rainbow Colours

White as a sheet,
Blue as the sea,
Black as liquorice,
Green as a pea.

Orange as an orange,
Red as blood,
As red as a ruby,
Brown as mud.

Yellow as the sun,
Brown as a wallet,
Blue as the Earth,
Orange as a mallet.

Purple like an aubergine,
White as a whiteboard,
Black like ink,
Multicoloured like a skateboard.

Orange as lava,
Pink as a pig,
Green as the grass,
Grey like an elephant, isn't it big?

William Ozzy Winterbotham (8)
Little Ealing Primary School

Seasons

The last golden summer's day
Is just starting to fade away
Before the blustery autumn breeze
Takes away the leaves from trees
Followed by the winter's cold frost
Now all leaves and flowers are lost
Butterflies and daffodils are in sight
Spring is here and back is the light.

Saskia Ernestine (11)
Little Ealing Primary School

Beautiful World

(Inspired by 'Beautiful World' by Take That)

Beautiful world
Make it last
Beautiful world
It goes so fast

Beautiful world
It is our home
Beautiful world
You're not alone

Beautiful world
In every hour
Beautiful world
Save some power

I am a beautiful world
Look after me
I am a beautiful world
Please let me be . . .

Emma Humphrey (10)
Little Ealing Primary School

Colours

As brown as a trunk
As blue as the sky
As white as a cloud
As black as a piece of coal
As gold as a piece of solid gold
As red as an apple
As grey as a dolphin
As green as seaweed
As pink as a pink water bottle.

Jude Ellis-Jones (9)
Little Ealing Primary School

My Assembly

On my gosh, it's my assembly
I don't know what to do,
I've just come back from holiday
I can't be as good as you.

Oh my gosh, it's my assembly
I've got to look my best,
So when I stand up on the stage
I stand out from all the rest!

Oh my gosh, it's my assembly
I've got to be clear and loud,
My parents are in the back row
I want to make them proud.

Oh my gosh, it's my assembly
I'm standing here on the stage,
I've just forgot my second line
I need my script page.

Meera Purohit (8)
Little Ealing Primary School

Night-Night

I look at the time,
The clock's turned nine,

My mum takes my hand,
Leads me upstairs and . . .

I have a quick bath,
We both have a laugh,

Snuggled up in bed,
Then my mum said,

'As you've been so nice,
I'll sing you Edelweiss.'

At my mum I had one last peep,
Before I fell asleep.

Amy Carter (10)
Little Ealing Primary School

Spells Trouble

I always spell trouble
T r o u b l e
But one day I forgot it,
Whilst doing a spelling Bee.

I was doing very well,
Mrs Lune asked me to spell it,
T r o b-
Bing! echoed the bell.

'Wrong, you're out!'
Mrs Lune snorted,
I just stared,
'Fine!' I retorted,
Big mistake!

And that day I really did spell . . . *T r o u b l e!*

Zoë Winterbotham (10)
Little Ealing Primary School

Secret Garden

Over the wall,
Through the gate
In the garden
You can't await
The mosaic patterns
All over the floor
And the school next door
The tall high plants
Spiralling here and there
The small, spring, pretty flower bed
The secret garden.

Joe Dinnage (9)
Little Ealing Primary School

My Summer Holiday - Haikus

Summer holiday,
France, Pevensey, Lulworth Cove,
No school for six weeks.

Pools, lakes and rivers.
Fun, exciting, cool water.
Splash, swim, jump and dive.

Colourful markets,
Fruits, bread, cheese, music and toys.
Busy, bustling towns.

Trois orangina.
Crepe nutella or citron
Grand café au lait.

Air show in Eastbourne.
Fusciardis mint ice cream.
Sovereign Harbour.

Lulworth Cove, cold sea.
Chips and 99 ice cream.
Stony and sandy.

Durdle door, clear sea.
Amazing seaweed and fish,
Ice cream halfway up.

Swanage steam railway.
Sandy beach, salty water.
Big lobsters, huge crabs.

Exciting Weymouth,
Walk out far, it's still shallow,
Warm, wavy, fun sea.

Chesil beach, deep sea.
Round, smooth, translucent pebbles.
Anglers and sea birds.

Charmouth, lost sandals.
Fossil hunting, exciting.
Fool's Gold, ammonites.

Knoll beach in Studland.
Sandy beach and cool water.
Interesting boats.

Back to school again,
End of summer holiday,
New term, new teacher.

Jennie Connelly (8)
Little Ealing Primary School

Differences

Some eyes are green,
Some eyes are blue,
My eyes are brown.
How about you?

Some people are tall,
Some people are short,
I'm not that tall,
It doesn't matter, I was taught.

Some people have brown hair,
Some have blonde.
Some even dye their hair,
Of that, I'm not really fond.

Some people are young,
Some are old.
Some are middle-aged,
I was told.

Some people are sad,
Some are happy.
Some people are quiet,
Some are chatty.

Mia Leeks (10)
Little Ealing Primary School

The Rusty Old Windmill

The old, old windmill,
His rusty cogs churning in the smoky London air,
Like one who knows he's had his day,
The old, old windmill.

As the wind blows calmly,
New plants begin to grow,
The windmill smiles as he watches over them.

He sighs as he remembers the sights he has seen,
As he looks back on all the memories
And looks at the ripe grass.

His latticed, yellow arms circle in the sun
And look towards it as if he knows something that we do not,
He rests peacefully as he starts to lie down,
And his head sways, and he slowly falls.

Oscar Driver (9)
Little Ealing Primary School

Me And Cars

I like smelling burnt and toasted brakes
And melted rubber of tortured tyres.

I like watching bright yellow Lamborghinis
Go past my window on a Monday morning.

I like walking through a luxurious car show
With 800-brake horse-power cars.

I like touching the lightweight Titanium
wheels of a Pagani Zonda.

I like seeing an M3 in a showroom
With a carbon fibre roof.

I like listening to the roar of an Aston Martin DB5.

I like power sliding a stunning laser-blue Noble.

Samuel Swaine (9)
Little Ealing Primary School

Embarrassing

I went to my best friend's house
And I saw a little, tiny mouse
Its eyes seemed to be getting bolder
Then it started climbing on my shoulder!
I was laughing and laughing as it crawled down my back
How embarrassing was that?
It even started chewing my backpack!

The next day at school
I was such a fool as I tried to be cool
But then it all went wrong!
I was walking down the hallway
And I said, 'What a lovely day!'
But suddenly I fell over
And landed on someone's back
It was like a domino track!
How embarrassing was that?

Isabella Heaver (7)
Little Ealing Primary School

Spring Colours!

What is green?
The grass is green with daisies in-between.
What is blue?
The sky is blue with aeroplanes whizzing through.
What is white?
The clouds are white, it is a beautiful sight.
What is red?
A ladybird is red looking for its leafy bed.
What is brown?
The branches are brown making whispering sounds.
What is yellow?
The sun is yellow with a friendly face saying hello.
What is pretty?
Everything is pretty.

Roha Umar (9)
Little Ealing Primary School

Heavenly Dreams

Late at night, when I go to bed
On the pillow I lay my weary head

I go to a place where no one knows
What goes on, or how it goes

A land where there's no trouble or strife
A million light years from this life

A land of peace and tranquillity
Joyful people and harmony

Children playing up in the trees
The wind, a gentle perfumed breeze

Animals of all shapes and sizes
All of differing types and guises

Soft cotton-like clouds afloat
These we use as travel boats

Gently taking us for a ride
Admiring the views in our stride

A magical land where all can fly
With tropical birds, eye to eye

Rivers of chocolate, dark and light
Rainbows of colour, extreme and bright

An everlasting paradise
Anything's possible, just close your eyes

So tonight I shall meet you there
On the cotton wool clouds up in the air . . .

Shakeel Rahman (9)
Little Ealing Primary School

Dangerous Animals

Dangerous as a dog
Angry as an alligator
Nasty as a nanny goat
Gentle as a giraffe
Elegant as an elk
Rough as a rat
Orange as an orang-utan
Small as a spider

Attractive as an antelope
Naughty as a nit
Immature as an iguana
Mad as a monkey
Agile as an anaconda
Lazy as a lizard
Slimy as a snake.

George Andrew Wilson (8)
Little Ealing Primary School

Inside My Box

(Inspired by 'Magic Box' by Kit Wright)

Scrum-Bum the dog is . . .
Soft as a cloud,
Warm like the sun,
As cute as a baby.

My fairy is as . . .
Small as an ant
Slim as a role model,
And cool as a cat.

My friendship bracelet is . . .
As special as my life,
As pretty as a princess
And as happy as ever.

Inside my box, I have lots of wonderful things!

Adeline Ruby Wild (8)
Little Ealing Primary School

My Burglar

My burglar comes out at night so no one can see him,
He is called Mick,
He is my friend and he steals things and gives me them,
He is mean and scary to the police so they run away.

He is hiding so no one can see,
When the police come he hides,
They go past him and he is safe,
My burglar has a blue mask, black and white T-shirt
And leather boots.

James Strahan (9)
Little Ealing Primary School

Spiders

Eight-legged creatures living in a web
Eating flies all day, especially in May
They're really cool, I think they rule,
Creeping and crawling over your feet.
Can you guess what they are . . . ?
Spiders!

Big spiders, little spiders and different colours too,
Brown, grey and especially black.

Spiders!

Izaak Picton-Falk (8)
Little Ealing Primary School

The Colourful Poem

Colourful as a rainbow
Red as a bonfire
Yellow as a lemon
Green as the grass
Dark green as the oak tree
Brown as a dead dragon
Purple as rhubarb
Grey as a rainy cloud
Blue as the sky.

Joseph Gordon (9)
Little Ealing Primary School

Buzzing Bee

Buzz, buzz, that's all they do
Buzzing all over you!
They sting you
You cry out in pain
Showing a lot of strain!
There are dead bees on the train!
Some people like bees but definitely not me
Even a pea is better than a bee!

James Cabraal (8)
Little Ealing Primary School

Daffodils

D affodils are as bright as a shimmering sun,
A s smooth as silk,
F eel like velvet,
F eel like soft material,
O ver the grass,
D affodils are as beautiful as butterflies,
I think they are as pretty as a tiara,
L ying on an emerald-green cushion,
S o attractive on the throne.

Nuala Gallagher (9)
Little Ealing Primary School

Flowers

F lowers, all colours, all year round,
L ittle flowers growing from the ground.
O ld flowers dying every day,
W e want to help them as we say.
E very day when you go home,
R each for your water, not your phone.
S uper . . . your flowers are alive!

Hannah Lunt (9)
Little Ealing Primary School

Flowers

Daffodils are soft as a pillow
Don't have much scent
Daffodils are yellow as the sun
They come out in spring.

Zara Parsons (8)
Little Ealing Primary School

The Secret Garden

The plants in the garden are as green as emeralds.
The daffodils are as yellow as the sun.
The lavender smells as beautiful as a rose.

The door to the garden is a metal plant
Growing up straight.
The windows have metal roses growing up.

Dylan Keene (8)
Little Ealing Primary School

I Will Put In My Box . . .

(Based on 'Magic Box' by Kit Wright)

I will put in my box . . .

A snowman from Antarctica,
A special feather from Africa,
A rishka cycle from Bangladesh,
The Eiffel Tower from Paris
And a plate from China.

I will put in my box . . .
A yellow sunflower,
A red rose,
A yellow daffodil
And a purple tulip.

Nishat Ahmed (8)
Montem Primary School

A Teddy Called Eddie

One day a teddy called Eddie
Was not a very steady teddy
In the window of the shop.

Nobody would buy Eddie
Because he was not steady
Until one day a boy called Bill
Bought Eddie and put him on the till
Because Eddie was *acting* very still.

Bill was glad, but Eddie was sad
Because he had left all the fun in the shop.
Eddie looked back and like a jumping jack
He jumped back into the shop window!

Bill couldn't believe his eyes . . .
He was very surprised
That Eddie had turned into a jumping jack.
Eddie was glad that he was back
But he had to take some flack.
But he didn't mind because all were very kind
And that was the end of that . . .

Lauryn Robinson-Williams (8)
Montem Primary School

All Wound Up . . .

Winding up, wound up
Fate plots a twist,
Once the winding clock is wound
Time will unfold
Freely and how it wishes.

Be wary for what you wish,
Because when your clock is wound,
No one nor anything can stand in its way.

I wish for an adventure,
Only that can sate my thirst,
With my great longing I feel deeply cursed.

Ever winding until one day,
When fate sets me on my course,
I will obediently follow until either fate is satisfied
Or I am beat.

I now sense that my time has come,
My clock is all wound up,
Now it is all wound up,
My adventure can begin . . .

Bridget Geraghty (11)
Our Lady of Lourdes Primary School

. . . Me, A Fish . . .

A fish I would be,
Swimming so freely,
For they can travel with friends
Or completely alone,
Also they can be pretty or rare
Bur no one will care,

A fish I would be,
A fish I would be,

So many adventures,
A fish must have endured,
I wish so badly
I could swim amongst the smallest of shrimp,

A fish I would be,
A fish I would be,

As well as this,
No boundaries they have,
Only freedom can they see
Through the tremendous waters of the blue sea,

A fish I would be,
A fish I would be,

So many creatures,
A fish must see, whales, dolphins, starfish and many,
Many other inhabitants of the sea.

A fish I would be,
A fish I would be,

What would you be?

Hannah Burke (11)
Our Lady of Lourdes Primary School

A Cat As Me

A cat I would be if I got to choose
Furry and fluffy, soft and smooth
I want to have adventures:
Running wild, jumping high
Climbing trees
'Cause it's time to be free
Jumping from walls, being able to crawl
Anywhere, high or low
But as a cat, one thing I fear:
Water!
Far or near
I can travel to far lands
Maybe . . . the Caribbean, Paris,
Or even Rome
But as you know, a cat is a cat
And cats hate water
So let's keep away from water
And one other thing . . .
I want to be free
So no owner for me
I want to have fun
And I want to run from dogs!
Nine lives I have and I want to keep
And if I fall, I always land on four feet
But beware: I may look cute and innocent . . .
But I can scratch, so never underestimate us cats
Ever so tiny, ever so cute
But when I start to hiss
Keep away: *snap, snap!*
A cat I would be if I got to choose
Furry and fluffy, soft and smooth.

Hannah Fenlon (10)
Our Lady of Lourdes Primary School

Untitled

You run through the forest like a bolt of lightning,
Sometimes boastful,
Why are you prey?
Scratching through the ground,
Owl swooping down,
Do you know why?

Athletic you are
What is your prey?
Rabbit, mouse,
I wish I knew

How do you live as prey?
Do you know?
How long do we live compared to you?
I wish I knew.

Do you wish you were king of the jungle?
Why are you so boastful?
Why are you such a show-off?
I wish I knew
I wish I were like you.

Harry Davies (9)
Our Lady of Lourdes Primary School

Mythical Creatures

Dragons, dreams and daring deeds.
Mythical creatures all
Gleam and shimmer.
From the largest dragon to the smallest fairy
All beautiful
And equal with the same shine.
Dragons, dreams and daring deeds
Beauteous all
Through your dreams!

Angel Constantinou (9)
Our Lady of Lourdes Primary School

When I'm High

I've always wanted to be a lion,
Jump so high, stoop so low,
Pounce to and fro.

I've always wanted to be a lion,
Indent into my prey,
Sink my teeth into its skin.
Blood as cold as an ice rink.

I've always wanted to be a lion,
Because if I were,
No one would mess with me.
I'd just impress.

My idea of being a lion is so lame . . .
But imagine it in a picture frame!

Renee Sagua (11)
Our Lady of Lourdes Primary School

What Am I?

What am I?
A fish
A monkey
A lion?
I just can't decide!
What am I?
There are loads to choose from
I could be as fast as lightning
Or I could wrestle other animals
I could scrape the human body
And blood would drop down my skin.
What am I?
Who knows?

Liam Lawrence (9)
Our Lady of Lourdes Primary School

My Wish Upon A Star

My wish upon a star,
Dark but true,
Is that my little related devil,
Goes far away
From me and you.

He laughs ridiculously,
Burps uncontrollably,
And makes rude gestures at the table.

He's rude to his vulnerable parents,
Farts in our faces too,
These are a couple of reasons,
That's why I want him away from me and you.

He has a bad habit,
Which really sucks,
Of leaving his sweaty judo gear on the floor,
While I pick it up,
My momma would say,
'Pick up your dirty clothes and put them away!'

But I know he's young,
Smiling true,
That's why he's here,
For me and you!

Anike Oye (10)
Our Lady of Lourdes Primary School

Horse!

Horses are like forces,
Galloping all around.

Having to get ready,
And unready.

Horses are like forces,
Cantering all around.

Being washed and dried,
Guiding his way to his stall.

Horses are like forces,
Trotting all around.

Taken out to the field,
As though he has been healed.

Horses are like forces,
Walking all around.

Emily Daly (10)
Our Lady of Lourdes Primary School

Puppy

Little and brown,
Jumping up and down,
Rolling around,
On the ground,
With small little ears,
That flop side to side,
With a small black nose,
Which is always wet,
Cute little eyes,
That watch the flies,
As she runs around with all her friends,
So if I were an animal, I would be a puppy!

Daniela Nolan (10)
Our Lady of Lourdes Primary School

Long Time Ago

A long time ago,
In the middle of a huge meadow,
Lived a woman,
Who was married to a Dutchman.
Several children they had,
But all of them were bad.
She never set foot out of the house,
And all her children wanted a mouse.
Even though she was scared of mice,
She was always extremely nice.
'It shall be,' she did say,
'On one condition; it must stay in the hay.'
So they got what they wanted,
Even though the woman thought it horrid.
The woman would always hide,
So the children had to keep the mouse outside.
Outside the mouse did die,
But the woman would always deny
That she had crept outside,
To kill the mouse; it had already died!

Ellie Dunning (11)
Our Lady of Lourdes Primary School

Tarantula

Tarantula big, tarantula strong,
Tarantula stings you and your heart goes *bong!*
No one likes 'em, no one goes near,
'I am going to kill you,' they all sneer!

Phoebe McMullan (8)
Rainbow Montessori School

The Sun

Hot, fiery and warm,
Burning in yellow all over the universe,
A giant star floating around space,
Waking and warming in the morning,
Covered by the moon in its eclipse,
Out in the day and inside at night,
Making rainbows in the rain,
Making solar power and making people happy,
Orange like our teacher's hair,
Bossy to the moon and a few stars like a mother,
Lighting the world in its colour,
Giving the Earth not too much light,
Stronger than any light,
Gold but not solid,
Fully made of gas,
Gives a good sight but don't look too close,
Or you'll get knocked out,
Shiny and stripy,
Making the moon shine in the night,
Making the sky very blue and making the clouds quite white,
Making the Earth have us humans,
Helping plants to make their food,
Making cold-blooded things move,
A big round ball,
Deadly if it's too close,
Son of the Big Bang,
Which was like an exploding frying pan,
It has lots of radiation
But as all of us humans know, it is too hot
For all of us to live on top,
Now you see how the sun is!

Ben Mizrahi (9)
Rainbow Montessori School

Hallowe'en

On the night, on Hallowe'en Day,
We will come and scare you all away.
Witches, ghosts and goblins too,
Although we are quite a few.
But if you still don't think we're scary,
We will turn you into a berry.
Witches have pointy hats,
And fly around with scary cats.
Racing on brooms through the sky,
Bringing fear to people's eyes.
But when the sun shines bright,
Every spooky thing will hide.
No longer will they be seen,
Until the next Hallowe'en!

Jordan Cohen (10) & Amalie Reitan (11)
Rainbow Montessori School

Just You And Me

Something has gone.
Gone away and I think it's you.
Come on, we'll go as far away as possible.
We'll grow wings and fly towards the clouds,
Just you and me!
Nobody telling us what to do,
And best of all, no fighting included.
Who knows what we'll find up there?
Maybe, we'll find a whole new life.
Don't be scared, hold my hand and wings will grow
And we'll fly up there, just you and me!

Zelda Feldman (8)
Rainbow Montessori School

Why?

Why is the universe big and black
And why do people talk so much?
Why is the world so big and round?
Why do people think so much
And why is there evil and good?

But why does the universe exist?
And why do people live and die?
Why? Why? Why?
Why? Why? Why?
Why? Why? Why?

Elmo Spethmann (10)
Rainbow Montessori School

Day

In the morning
When the sun is yawning
Later in the day
When the sun shines like May
And in the evening when the sun is red
I get ready to go to bed.
Now far into the night,
We are all sleeping very tight.

Lavinia Carey (9)
Rainbow Montessori School

Pure Love

Tulips are red
Just like love.
And you never know that red
Is just like a dove.
The sky is blue,
And I'm so happy that I have you.
I love you, my bunny,
And you are as sweet as honey.
I give you my flowers and love.
I love you, my boy,
You give me joy.
I love you my girl,
You are the best one in the world!

Katerina Forrest (7)
Rainbow Montessori School

My Wish

If I had a wish
It would be
To fly across the galaxy.
If I had a wish,
I'd wish to have super powers
And save the world.
I'd be pleased
If I had a wish.
I'd wish to be
A pop star singing
The songs that people love.
That would be my wish.

Leela Barlow (8)
Rainbow Montessori School

The Ocean

I wish I could see
Under the surface of the sea,
I just know there's a wonder
Under the deep blue water.

One day I'll explore
The ocean floor,
I will bring back the treasure
And all will gather
To see . . .

Clara Sibaud (11)
Rainbow Montessori School

Trees

I climbed up a tree
What a peaceful place to be
Sitting under a nest
Is the place I like to rest.

Lilyella Zender-Blatt (9)
Rainbow Montessori School

I'm Computer Mad

I'm computer mad,
It's not that bad,
Except that it refuses to work with me,
But it's not as annoying as when my cat has fleas!

Dulcie Fowler (8)
Rainbow Montessori School

Water

Water, the slippery surface glistening in the sun
The brilliant turquoise world seems to be alive
As its waves breathe
Just like you and me

Water, its beautiful flow drawing people closer
They sit down, eating and playing beside it
And when they are finished
They throw their waste, ruining its beauty

Water, the creatures inside it suffering
The toxic waste slowly decaying their bodies
You can sense their screams
Even though you cannot hear them

Water, it will get revenge
We humans will soon be slaughtered
Just like the creatures within
As the water we drink is no different from the water we poison!

Hannah Darling (11)
Ravenscourt Park Preparatory School

Death And Destruction

Fish are dying from oil spills
Elephant tusks are being pulled
The trees are cut down and killed
Coral is destroyed
Garden birds are becoming rarer
While polar bears' homes are melting down.
How can we save the world?

Joe Grieve (10)
Ravenscourt Park Preparatory School

Our World

Our world, planet Earth,
The third rock from the sun.
The world that has been given to us,
And belongs to everyone.

Our world, planet Earth,
The third rock from the sun,
With the deer that leaps and the bear that hunts
And rests when it is done.

Our world, planet Earth,
The third rock from the sun.
With mountains and forests that rise from the sky,
And ice caps where Arctic wolves run.

Our world, planet Earth,
The third rock from the sun,
And when we have destroyed it,
There will not be another one.

Harry Coke (10)
Ravenscourt Park Prepatory School

Our World

The fish, the animals, the trees, the birds
And the sweet meadow breeze,
Buffaloes grazing in the fields
And birds singing in the trees.
The sea like polished glass
And the skies like a blanket of blue.
Snow-capped mountains
And fast jungles too.

Toby Clyde (10)
Ravenscourt Park Preparatory School

More Than A Danger

Global warming is described as horrific,
horrendous, ghastly, life-threatening and sorrowful.

According to people, the ice caps will melt,
flooding everything that lies too low.

Newspapers tell us in big, bold writing, *we shall die.*
Our descendants will wake up knowing they are going to die.

But do humans care? The answer is yes, they do.
They do not want many organisms to die.

However, that want is not big enough.
Many people would prefer to be slouching on the sofa
rather than protesting against a Heathrow expansion.

So this is more than a danger, it's impossible to describe.
How are we going to get anywhere with people
who want to watch 'The Simpsons' rather than save the world?

Oscar Mayhew (11)
Ravenscourt Park Preparatory School

Polar Bears

The gale blows hard,
Fighting its way through the threatening snow.
The polar bears hibernate in the dark,
And all the animals lie low.

The polar bears cuddle their cubs lovingly,
Diving for seals.
The mother brings one up happily
And keeps it for their meal.

But now we are losing the bears bit by bit;
Soon there will be nothing left.
There will be nowhere for them to sit:
What is the cause of this theft?

Anna Kerr (11)
Ravenscourt Park Preparatory School

The Wonderful Animals Are Dying

The tough, powerful polar bears are slowly sinking into the cold
icy water.
As the endangered animals catch their fish
the snow beneath their heavy white bodies melts.
The wonderful animals are dying.

The brilliant trees are being chopped down,
As spectacular birds and monkeys flee from their homes,
in the hope that they will soon find another home.
The wonderful animals are dying.

The rivers and lakes are being filled with rubbish and chemicals.
As fantastic, shiny fish struggle to swim around, they get strangled
by the rubbish or poisoned by the chemicals they breathe.
The wonderful animals are dying!

Amelia Gosztony (11)
Ravenscourt Park Preparatory School

Endangered Animals

The tiger, the buffalo and more
All the animals on the forest floor
Are hunted for their skins and bone
Which will make us humans alone

The forest will be quiet and sad
If we continue our ways so bad
The world will be an unhappy place
If we don't change our ways in haste

So don't hunt the tiger, the buffalo and more
Or the animals on the forest floor
That way we will have our world to share
And show that we really care.

Oscar Jenkyn-Jones (10)
Ravenscourt Park Preparatory School

Birds

I swooped through the dense air, flying through a curtain of smoke,
Exhaust fumes wafted in the air, suffocating plumes,
The sky was a damp, grey dishcloth that was draped over Earth,
They paved a paradise!

Smoke, big black clouds of it, bellowed out of the factories,
Litter loomed over the land, great towers of shrivelled paper, glass
and sharp metals,
They paved a paradise,.

Vats of toxic waste illuminated the gloom,
A grey cloud that would hang over Earth, our Earth for evermore,
They paved a paradise!

Rain plummeted from the sky,
Hitting the Earth that had been stripped bare of forest and
animals' land,
Now I miss the blades of emerald grass that used to grow,
They paved a paradise!

Trees will grow no longer,
The sky, always dark,
My heart, always filled with sorrow,
They paved my paradise!

Elsa Darlington (10)
Ravenscourt Park Preparatory School

When The Ice Melts

When the ice melts from the polar caps,
Polar bears will be no longer,
The silky, white fur will vanish forever,
Graceful beasts, never to be remembered,
Never again, never again!

When the ice melts from the polar caps,
The world will be flooded,
Life wiped out by gushing water,
Oceans will rise,
Life will sink,
Covered by water, covered by water!

When the ice melts from the polar caps,
The damage caused,
We cannot rebuild,
Nothing will survive,
Nothing, nothing!

When the ice melts from the polar caps,
We will not be there to see the destruction,
Washed away with everything else,
Our pollution will be our destruction,
All our fault, all our fault!

Adam Plavsic (11)
Ravenscourt Park Preparatory School

The Oil

Its means of flight,
Its means of sight,
Drowned by the oil.
Lost, lost, lost.

The tanker sinks,
Into the water it drinks.

Its wings are glued,
It is now food,
For the oil to eat,
To eat, to eat, to eat.

The tanker sinks,
Into the water it drinks.

So why kill our world?
Our beautiful, glorious world.
So why kill our world?
Why kill it? Why kill it? Why kill it?

Hugo French (9)
Ravenscourt Park Preparatory School

Look After Our World

Dear, oh dear, stop global warming
For all the animals it's torturing.
Ice caps melting, animals dying.
We all feel remorse.

Humanity killing, animals suffering.
Illegal hunting continues
And cars give off fumes every day.

The fumes - stop them!
Non-electric cars - stop them!
Hunting - stop it!
It's our world,
If you look after it, it will look after you.

Stanley Love (11)
Ravenscourt Park Preparatory School

Dolphins

Ripples in the ocean,
A dolphin appears.
Not in the future
Unless my message the world hears.

Ripples in the ocean,
A dolphin breaks free.
Is there anyone in the world who cares
Or is it just me?

Ripples in the ocean,
A dolphin chirps a song.
Why do you kill them
And not think it's wrong?

Ripples in the ocean,
A dolphin swims on.
They'll die away some day,
Going, going, *gone* . . .

Anna Burnett (10)
Ravenscourt Park Preparatory School

3008

Why use these gas-filled tanks,
when you can cycle along the banks
and watch and listen to the birds?
I can't even put it into words.

As for paper, use both sides
follow the recycling guides.
You won't believe how many trees
go into making tons of these.

If we want our world to stay the same
we must help before we're to blame.
Turn off the lights before it's too late,
don't destroy our world by 3008!

Ella Burdett (10)
Ravenscourt Park Preparatory School

Selfishness

Numbers descending, hunters ascending,
How can animals survive
When they have no home?
How can they have an easy life,
When all they own is crushed to dust by giant bulldozers?
Are we making too much progress,
For our beautiful world to survive?
Do we relish destroying animals' homes?
Houses ascending, wildlife descending,
Is this the world we want to live in?
Do we want every beautiful creature to become extinct because
of our selfishness?

Houses descending, wildlife ascending,
This is the way it should be.

Gregor Fuller (10)
Ravenscourt Park Preparatory School

The Sea

The sea,
A deep, mysterious blue,
The waves gently lap at the sandy, yellow shore,
And down, down in the depths where no man roams,
Another world,
Colourful and nature a-plenty,
But . . .
We didn't think, we didn't care,
We polluted the sea with waste and dirty air,
Lives are lost,
The sea turns black,
Drained of life itself,
Oh the sea, oh the sea,
It has gone, it has gone!

Eliza Baring (9)
Ravenscourt Park Preparatory School

Our Beautiful World

The luscious, green, graceful grass,
is swaying swiftly in the breeze.
The flourishing flowers are colourful,
and so are the rich, ripe apple trees.
The calm contented animals stride through the grass,
up high, fly the birds and bees.

We are happy with our peaceful world,
so we are not very hard to please.
But God, please take pity on us,
help us have a blissful, healthy world forever.
To keep it tidy, neat and clean,
and to sweep . . . sweep away the mean.

Help us look after our world, our world, our world.
Help us look after our world!

Amelia Lloyd (10)
Ravenscourt Park Preparatory School

The Last Tree

The last tree stood, withered and old,
Its leaves were grey and its branches cold.
Soon its branches were rotten and black
Touch it and its bough might crack.
The leaves floated down, one by one,
Rotting in the scorching sun.
Its blackened bark was cracked and raw
The last tree, my last tree, the last tree
I ever saw.

Maisie Cowell (9)
Ravenscourt Park Preparatory School

Poem

The ice caps melting,
the polar bears sinking,
because we're not aware
we are murdering the polar bear.

The ice caps melting,
the polar bears sinking,
the cars flying by
making the polar bears die.

The ice caps melting,
the polar bears sinking,
the fossil fuels burning
and the oceans rising.

The ice caps melting,
the polar bears sinking.
If we don't do anything now
we will never see these incredible creatures again.

The ice caps melting,
the polar bears sinking,
the gasses are created
leaving the polar bears' fate in our own hands.

Harry Mayes (11)
Ravenscourt Park Preparatory School

Our World

Our world shan't die on its own,
We will kill it,
Let us stop and enjoy our world,
Forever we should love its grass,
Its sky,
Its waters,
The fumes destroy and crush our lives,
We may pass,
But let the world stay,
May we pray for our forgiveness,
Hope God pities us,
The flooding has started,
The weather has changed,
Animals die,
Trees vanish without trace,
Let it live,

Our world!

Luca Cericola (10)
Ravenscourt Park Preparatory School

The Lovely Elephant

An elephant, not a beast
But men come and feast
On its white tusks that are made of bone
The poachers then sell them at the market
We should look after the animals
They are friends not foes
They are like our family
Not to kill them but to admire them
If we do not kill them
They can walk among us
As our friends
We can look after them.

Alexander Fassone (10)
Ravenscourt Park Preparatory School

The Environment

You cannot return what is gone
You cannot replace what is gone

The cheetah's sprint
The bird's glide

You cannot return what is gone
You cannot replace what is gone

The polar bear's roar
The kangaroo's jump

You cannot return what is gone
You cannot replace what is gone

The mouse's squeak
And the dolphin's chatter

What is gone
Is always gone!

Alex Pigott (9)
Ravenscourt Park Preparatory School

Pandas

Pandas are becoming extinct,
They will live in China all alone,
The mountainside is their home.
Pandas are big and tall.
But they are peaceful and gentle and don't fight at all.
They eat bamboo shoots all day long.
They are calm . . . and in our world they belong.

Lizzie Bramley (9)
Ravenscourt Park Preparatory School

Just Remember The Polar Bear

We need to look after the polar bears,
The brilliant white beasts,
Treading through the crunchy snow,
Looking for a feast.

But their icy home is getting warmer,
It's turning to sea, not snow,
And if we continue polluting the world
All the polar bears will go.

The polar bears are endangered,
We've got to look after their home,
And if we don't, the results will be
They'll have no place to wander, no place to roam.

So look after the environment,
We can all do our little bit,
Just remember the polar bear, remember its home,
We have to look after it!

Emma Olrik (9)
Ravenscourt Park Preparatory School

Beautiful World

So many beautiful animals on Earth,
Mammals, reptiles, birds and amphibians.
It's their world as well as ours,
Let's share this world with them.
The deep blue waters, the shining sands,
The clear sky up above.
These, too, we must look after, otherwise they will be gone.
We have to start to think about the animals that we live with,
Because otherwise they will be one stop closer to extinction.
Deforestation, over-fishing and pollution are all threats to them.
Let's give these animals one more chance,
After all it's their world as well as ours.

Imogen Cunningham (10)
Ravenscourt Park Preparatory School

We Must Care For Our Beautiful World

Do we really care about our beautiful world?
We should.

Look at what is happening.
Factories burning coal faster than we can think.
People dumping their rubbish into the canals every day.
Carbon dioxide mounting in the atmosphere.
The clouds turning grey.
Trees disappearing like wood on fire.

But we can change this and save,
Plains and plains of green, green grass.
The delicate flowers swaying in the breeze.
Birds whistling and tweeting like a flute.
The predators roaring like foghorns.

We can stop this.
Will you help?
The future is in our hands.

Matthew Piercy (9)
Ravenscourt Park Preparatory School

We Must Care For Our Beautiful World

We must care for our beautiful world
Or into the depths of darkness it will be hurled.
All the plants, trees and animals
Are being devoured by bulldozers, the cannibals!
As the moon rises yellow, in the sky,
He hears the animals cry,
'Save us! Save us! Save us now!'
But the moon only replies, 'How?'
Man has paved nature's wonderland
With concrete, tarmac and sand.
We must care for our beautiful world
Or into the depths of darkness it will be hurled.

Alexander Rugman (9)
Ravenscourt Park Preparatory School

A Bare, Lonely World

Trees are cut down,
cars roll by,
factories pump out smoke,
like a heart pumping fast,
leaving a bare, lonely world.
All the mountains of snow,
as white as a polar bear,
melt rapidly in the heat,
They will all go, soon go.
Wheels roll by, leaving grass
as flat as flat can be,
like lily pads on the ground,
not swaying in the water.
Trees are cut down,
cars roll by,
factories pump out smoke,
like a heart, pumping fast,
leaving a bare, lonely world.

Charlotte Stapleton (9)
Ravenscourt Park Preparatory School

Our World

Our world has cars,
What does that do?
Our world has planes,
What does that do?
Pollution, pollution,
It kills our entire world,
It kills people,
It kills you.
If you don't drive a car to work
But cycle or walk to work,
You are a hero!
So plant more trees and walk to school,
And don't drive your car to work!

Joe Lister (8)
Ravenscourt Park Preparatory School

We Must Care For Our Beautiful World

Do we really care about our world
And all the animals that we are endangering?
The polar bear is one of these poor creatures.
Its paws can't find any ice to break.
Its prey is disappearing at the speed of an ice cube
Melting in the sun.
Its powerful body is turning weak with the heat.
Long ago, before this disaster happened,
They would roam around as free as a bird,
But now this disaster has struck
We need to stop making better fuel-guzzling cars
That will melt the Arctic
And make a difference for this animal
Or there will be no more polar bears in the world.
And it will be our fault, not theirs.
So are you going to make a difference
Or are you going to let this animal die?
Its future is in our hands . . .

Finn Brown (9)
Ravenscourt Park Preparatory School

My Dream Of The Endangered Polar Bear

In my dream of the polar bear,
I see him standing strong and proud.
He swims with force,
He swims with grace,
His fearsome paws making massive waves.
His eyes are blue,
His eyes are sharp,
At night his eyes twinkle like stars.
His fur is thick,
His fur is white,
He needs his fur to stay warm at night.
His powerful jaw is full of razor-sharp teeth,
But they get almost nothing to eat.
His world is cruel,
His world is harsh,
And I am afraid his world won't last!

Ella Lindsay (9)
Ravenscourt Park Preparatory School

What Is The World?

What is the world?
The world once was peace, where dinosaurs roamed,
over the green, green grass.
Nevermore, nevermore.

What is the world?
The world is crowded, poisoned by death, war and extinction,
For evermore, for evermore.

What is Man?
Man once was peaceful, hardworking and beautiful,
Nevermore, nevermore.

What is Man?
Man is greedy, insolent and war-like,
For evermore.

What is the world?
What is the world?

Thomas Polyblank (10)
Ravenscourt Park Preparatory School

There Used To Be A Field Here

There used to be a field here.
Full of blossoming flowers and trees,
And the only noise that people could hear
Was the humming of birds and bees.

But they came along and dug it up
Every last blade of grass,
They built a massive factory
With its chimney, an upside-down vase.

I really prefer a shimmering field
To a factory pumping out smoke
There used to be a meadow here
It's a factory now - it's no joke.

Hope Coke (9)
Ravenscourt Park Preparatory School

Don't Drop Litter Everywhere

Don't drop litter everywhere
it stinks,
it looks awful,
why do people do it?
People do it because
they're too lazy
to find a bin
and drop it in.
People leave beer cans
everywhere and
it smells like beer
around every corner.
Why leave
half-eaten junk food on the ground?
If you do that
you are a pig.
Don't drop litter anywhere, it stinks!

Freddie Foulkes (8)
Ravenscourt Park Preparatory School

My Dog

My dog had the flu,
I didn't know what to do.
He wouldn't take his pill.
He became more ill.
I felt sad.
I felt mad.
If he had died,
I would have cried.
Now he's playing in the sun,
Having lots and lots of fun!

Ellen Smith (9)
St Ann's CE Primary School, Tottenham

Lunchtime

It is lovely lunchtime,
I'm choosing my fantastic food.
Today I choose perilous pasta
With spicy spaghetti.
I also fetch wonderful water
Which refreshes me like ice.
I have some crunchy crackers
And bitter butter with chunky cheese.
Walking out to the playground, I see grey gravel.
As boring as standing outside alone, doing nothing.
I smack the bowled ball for six.
Soon the booming bell rings, oh no!

Adeyemi Adeola (9)
St Benedict's Junior School, Ealing

My Big Sister

She's a talkative telly,
She's an uncomfortable chair.
A pufferfish ready to blow up.
A big giraffe.
She's a small town with lots of ideas,
She's cold like Russia.
A big mouth megaphone,
A buzzing alarm.
She's a late evening fox,
She's a sister waking you up!

Bogdan de Berg (10)
St Benedict's Junior School, Ealing

Autumn Walk

We trudged through the crunchy leaves,
Red, yellow, green and orange.
We saw a mellow sunlight shine
Through the black, gigantic, monstrous trees,
With 901,050 arms,
Like silhouettes against the bright sunlight.
Soggy, squelchy, waterlogged and lawn-patched grass.
Nature had shut down
And gone to sleep.
Animals were scurrying around,
Putting their finishing touches
On their underground nests.

Tristan Jenkin-Gomez (8)
St Benedict's Junior School, Ealing

Glory To God

Glory be to God for the wonderful trees
That breeze in the refreshing wind.
Thank You for the thunder that flashes and crackles
In the pitch-black night.
Thank You for all the dark blue sea,
With all the splashing dolphins,
And whales that swim joyfully with glee.
Thank You for the smashing and crashing waterfalls,
And for the sunrise that rises into the light blue sky,
With birds that are as colourful as a rainbow.
Thanks be to God for the wonderful world.
Praise Him.

Oliver Buchanan (9)
St Benedict's Junior School, Ealing

My Noisy Family

My family are the noisiest people you could ever meet.
The walls of our house quiver and shiver
with the sound of their stamping feet.
We are the noisiest family in the street!

At night I find it hard to sleep
and very often have to creep
downstairs to pinch the hairy nose
of my dad to stop his snoring, I suppose.

Grandad Bill starts the day
with his digger in our garden bay.
Sister Susie slams her door
and makes our Grandma Murray drop to the floor.

Brother Joey always storms
up and down as he performs
each day on his bounding drums
that shake and rattle all our mums.

And now I have finally had enough
as Uncle Ted has had a huff,
while watching Man U on our TV
and screams and shouts and makes me believe
that it is time to leave.

So if you see me sitting still
don't disturb me. As I will be so tranquil
quietly sitting in my favourite place,
away from the chatter and noise,
and ready to embrace
my favourite home, the library,
a place that I can face!

Olivia Smith (9)
St Benedict's Junior School, Ealing

Ten Brothers

Ten brothers went out to dine,
One choked on his food,
And then there were nine.

Nine brothers went to see their mate,
One went down a hole,
And then there were eight.

Eight brothers went to Heaven,
One stayed,
And then there were seven.

Seven brothers bought cheese sticks,
One bought too little and faded away,
And then there were six.

Six brothers went for a drive,
One brother crashed,
And then there were five.

Five brothers bought a door,
The door fell on one brother,
And then there were four.

Four brothers went to see an oak tree,
And the tree collapsed on one brother,
And then there were three.

Three brothers went to the hospital
Because they had flu,
One didn't survive,
And then there were two.

Two brothers went to see their mum,
One stayed,
And then there was one.

One brother,
Was left with no one to play with,
So he jumped off the cliff for fun,
And then there were none!

Sam Scott (10)
St Benedict's Junior School, Ealing

November

November, I just love you,
November, you are great!
You stop me feeling down or blue.
November, I can't wait!

November is a cold chap.
With Christmas not far off,
He wears a rug upon his lap,
To prevent a winter cough.

The leaves fall off everywhere,
All crispy, brown or red.
It's like November's losing his hair,
He's quietly in his bed.

November has a magic coat,
Made from unicorn hair!
He looks a lot like a billy goat.
He wears it *everywhere!*

He's mad just like a firework,
Since Bonfire Night's nearby!
The noise drives dogs berserk!
He's amazing, he can fly!

November, I just love you,
November, you are great!
You stop me feeling down or blue.
November, I can't wait!

Rory Hobson (11)
St Benedict's Junior School, Ealing

The Track

Enormous elephants explore
Along the echoing track

Mischievous monkeys meander
Along the messy track

Powerful panthers prowl
Along the pebbly track

Slimy snakes slither
Along the stony track

Terrible tigers trek
Along the tricky track

The echoing,
Messy,
Pebbly,
Stony and
Tricky track
Leads
The enormous elephants,
The mischievous monkeys,
The powerful panthers,
The slimy snakes and
The terrible tigers
To the
River!

Theodore Hyams (7)
St Benedict's Junior School, Ealing

My Big, Jolly Family!

My sister is three and a half, we like to joke in the bath
and she really makes me laugh

My mum is always so fun and is always happy, never glum,
and has rosy cheeks the colour of a plum

My dad is a great smelly lad and always glad
and I can't remember a time when I have seen him mad

My furry cat is really fat and I can never move her
from her dirty mat

I have twenty-two cousins who live all around
except for one for lives out of town

And finally, I have eight pretty aunties
who just love going to parties.

Francesca O'Neill (9)
St Benedict's Junior School, Ealing

My Friend Richard

He's a talkative telly,
He's a lively cheetah
And a roaring lion.
He's a town by the sea.
He's a fire alarm waiting to go off.
A fantastic Friday lunch.
A bullet flying down the rugby pitch.
That's my friend.

Charlie Sanderson (10)
St Benedict's Junior School, Ealing

Farmer Ben

There once was a man called Ben
Who loved to look after a hen
He had a wife called Ellie
Who said Ben was smelly
Because Ben didn't wash his belly

One day when Ben opened the gate
To feed his hen off a plate
The hen let out a squawk
When it saw a knife and fork . . .
Because hens only like to eat pork!

Liam Carty-Howe (8)
St Benedict's Junior School, Ealing

My Dad Is Mad!

My dad, he's mad!
He eats the newspaper instead of reading it.
He spreads marmalade on his cornflakes.
He puts toast in the kettle.
He polishes his shoes with bananas
And pours orange juice in his bowl at breakfast.

He's mad, my dad!

Toby McDonald (8)
St Benedict's Junior School, Ealing

Night

I met at eve the Lady of Night,
Tiptoeing from star to star,
Smiling at me with her gentle face
When I heard her call from afar.

Her hazel hair hung tousled,
Her dark eyes watching over me,
She kept me safe from nightmares
That was plain for me to see.

The Lady of Night rests on the moon
She is hidden away before the shine of noon,
She wears grey colours for she has no feelings,
Though she cares for others beyond their believings.

I met at eve the Lady of Night,
Tiptoeing from star to star,
Smiling at me with her gentle face
When I heard her call from afar.

Evie Gracie-Barnes (10)
St Benedict's Junior School, Ealing

Glory To God

Glory to God for His creation,
The trees that swirl in the wind,
The fire that crackles with the coal.
When the water sprays in your face,
When you swim with the waves.
The snow that sparkles in the sunlight,
And most of all the Earth.
Praise Him, praise Him!

Joshua Wood (10)
St Benedict's Junior School, Ealing

Who Night Really Is

Night is kind and caring,
She makes me feel light.
She is a bit daring,
That's why she holds me tight.

She looks at me warmly,
With a big, blurry face.
She is quite smart, surely,
Until she goes back to base.

Her eyes are a diamond of blue,
But when she floats off,
A bad dream goes *boo!*
And I start to cough.

Her teeth are perfectly normal,
Her hair is short and blonde.
Her voice sounds abnormal,
And she lives near a pond.

Stelios Souvaliotis (11)
St Benedict's Junior School, Ealing

Glory To God

Glory to God for all our gifts,
The sun that sparkles in the day
And never burns out.
Shining sand where the water
Shimmers in the light.
Thank You for the planets
We can see at night.
But most of all,
Thank You for me.
Thanks be to God for the
Wonderful world.
Praise Him.

Francis Curran (10)
St Benedict's Junior School, Ealing

November

I met November in the still of the night,
Whilst the snow was falling down,
On his head I saw a sight,
A jewel-encrusted crown.

November's eyes were like two green emeralds,
His hair was long and brown,
November's face showed no emotions,
His mouth was nothing but a frown.

November was wearing a jet-black shirt,
His torn shorts came up to his knees,
Ankle-high boots were on his feet
And he was carrying a bunch of keys.

November's house was completely ruined,
It all looked very dreary,
But when he opened the door with the keys,
It all became rather cheery.

Inside the house there was a burning fire,
That kept me very warm,
All of a sudden I fell asleep,
I didn't wake up until dawn!

Oliver Clark (11)
St Benedict's Junior School, Ealing

Night

Night is nasty, scary yet lonely.
Night brings nightmares into your mind.
His eyes burn black
And his hair dangles like cobwebs in the breeze.

Night glides along the ground.
He is alone, alone, all on his own.
No friends, no family, no one, he is alone . . .

Christy Creighton (11)
St Benedict's Junior School, Ealing

Snow, Snow, Everywhere

Snow, snow, everywhere,
Over here, over there.
It's very cold
And one week old,
Snow, snow, everywhere.

Skiers, skiers everywhere,
Whooshing here, flying there.
Down the slope,
Up the lift.
Oh no! That man
Went over the cliff.

Skiers, skiers everywhere,
Whooshing here, flying there.
Sometimes happy,
Sometimes sad,
Sometimes kicking and hitting their dads.

Guy McDonald (9)
St Benedict's Junior School, Ealing

My Best Friend

My best friend is a crazy baboon.
He's a bouncing ball,
He's a jumping banana.
My best friend is a cool type of car.
I don't know what will become of him,
But he's still my best chum!

Samuel Jury (9)
St Benedict's Junior School, Ealing

Autumn

As I stepped,
Out of the warm, cosy school,
I felt the cold icy breeze against my face.
The trees were bare
And the mellow sun shone deeply
Behind trees, making them black as soot.
The grass was muddy and sludgy
Great for slide races and mud fights.
We looked at our wobbly reflection
In a ripply, shallow puddle.
As we went into school,
The warmth hit me again.

Thomas Zussman (7)
St Benedict's Junior School, Ealing

Greedy Rhonda

One day there was a cute girl,
Who had hair with a cute curl.
She liked to drink tea,
But not with me.
She ate a chocolate cat
That made her very fat.
She ate some chocolate mice
and then ate some chocolate rice.
She saw the colour red
And then she dropped dead.

Daniel Michael (9)
St Benedict's Junior School, Ealing

Fishing

Fishing is really great
Especially with a good mate
Trout and carp
You catch on something quite sharp,
Maggots and worms are brilliant bait,
So you can catch fish which is great!
Reeling and casting
I'm still mastering,
So I guess that's right
They put up a great fight!

Tiernan Sheehan (11)
St Benedict's Junior School, Ealing

Dad

I've got this dad you see,
This is how he looks to me.
He's a little bit fat
And a little bit scary
A little bit tall,
And a little bit hairy.
He wears a baseball cap
Which is a tiny bit sad,
But, oh well!
I love my dad!

Chay Siu (10)
St Benedict's Junior School, Ealing

Night

Night is scary
Trust me I've seen her
Her hair is black and glossy
Her eyes are like the moon, all aglow.

She has no friends
Too scary is she
She is slick - so fast
With her black cape flowing behind.

Black lips
Decaying teeth
A cave is where she lives
With her pet mice, bats and spiders.

She makes you think bad things
A scary face is as blue as a river
She is a burglar
She steals your dreams and replaces them with nightmares.

Lucy Bartle (10)
St Benedict's Junior School, Ealing

My Sister

She's an uncomfortable chair,
She's a vicious lion ready to pounce.
She's Scotland in the winter,
She's a roaring lion at 3 o'clock in the morning.
She's a Monday, ready to go back to school,
But I have to put up with her!
OK!

James Porter (10)
St Benedict's Junior School, Ealing

Autumn

As we walk through the crunchy leaves,
Red and yellow, orange and green,
The chilly, soft, icy breeze
Blowing on our faces,
And the mellow sunlight shining
From monstrous trees,
Standing like giants with a hundred arms.
Walking through the soggy, squelchy grass,
Great for mud sliding and mud pies.
Nature has shut down for winter.
Animals scurry around underground,
Finishing their nests.
As we trudge on through the crunchy leaves,
We stop at a rippling puddle,
And wave at our reflection.

George Charlesworth (7)
St Benedict's Junior School, Ealing

Jack Spat

Jack Spat always ate fat
And all he could do was lie on a mat.
Jack ate on, until he was the size of a car.
'How long can this go on for?' cried his poor mama.
Along came his friend, little Tim Spouse,
By this time, he was the size of a house!
Soon poor Jack dropped down dead,
Clutching his ted called Fred!

William Davies (8)
St Benedict's Junior School, Ealing

So Silent

It was so silent I could hear . . .
ants working, helping the queen with her eggs,
an architect drawing a house,
a squirrel nibbling my leg,
my alarm clock ticking away my life.

I could hear . . .
a dog digging a hole for its bone,
a burglar sneaking into my house,
trees swaying in rhythm,
Big Ben's hands moving from then to now.

But then, suddenly,
we were under attack by Cyber Daleks
And Lasers were buzzing my house down!

I fell asleep!

Thomas Sanders (9)
St Benedict's Junior School, Ealing

About Me Poem

Hello everyone, my name is Sean
I'd like to tell you that from the day I was born
I've loved certain foods, particularly corn
I jump on my trampoline which is on the lawn
Sometimes I catch my jumper on a thorn
And it ends up getting very badly torn
My favourite seafood has to be prawn
And if I never eat another, I will be very forlorn.

Sean Anthony (8)
St Benedict's Junior School, Ealing

I Have A Pony In Me

I have a pony in me,
It trots and gallops all day long,
It feeds on hay, it never stops working,
It does not mind people,
It does not mind rain,
It does mind people if they are a pain.

I have a pony in me,
It jumps all day long,
I want to stroke it,
It's a beautiful, pretty bay, like chocolate.

I have a pony in me!

Ellie Scott (9)
St Benedict's Junior School, Ealing

Brothers

Brothers, brothers everywhere,
Fighting, biting, snoring, complaining.
When the rain is pouring,
Twirling, hurling, watching horror videos.
Sitting, staring, coming to blows.
But though my brothers are rather thin,
They can do a lot of sin.
I heard my mother quietly mutter
'Maybe daughters would have been better!'

Rachel de Cintra (8)
St Benedict's Junior School, Ealing

James Goes

(A cautionary tale)

People do bad things but James Goes
Picked his nose,
Until there was nothing left.
Although this was a criminal theft.
One very normal day
In the month of May
He got his finger stuck in there!
The whole town tried to get it out including the mayor
But with that, the poor little guy
Certainly did die!

George Johnson (9)
St Benedict's Junior School, Ealing

Miss Whales Bites Her Nails

There once was a lady called Miss Whales,
And she had a habit of biting her nails.
She met a boy called Bert,
And did you know he wore a skirt?
And then she met a king
And he had wings.
She bit her nails for such a long time
Eventually she tripped on a line.
She died from this fall,
Biting nails isn't for all.

Alex Mitchell-Bruguera (9)
St Benedict's Junior School, Ealing

The Prawn

The prawn is as crunchy as Crunchie bar
It is orange and it is curly and small
It smells fishy
It reminds me of the sea
A salty taste like fish
Smooth as a baby's skin
Some bits rough
To eat and try
Makes me feel hungry
It reminds me of my grandpa
He was a fishmonger.

Henry Goode (10)
St Benedict's Junior School, Ealing

Dad's Gone Mad

My dad is nice,
He doesn't like mice.
He has a hard chest
And doesn't make a mess.
He likes to drink beer
And he likes to cheer.
This is my dad,
He is absolutely mad!

William Poyntz (9)
St Benedict's Junior School, Ealing

The Sun

The sun shines on the sea
Like a beam of light hits a mirror.
It glistens against the snow
Like diamonds dazzling.
It is as yellow as a banana
And as orange as an orange.
It's as round as a tennis ball.
The sun is as hot as an oven,
A hot fireball.
The sun is a star in the night sky,
Millions of miles away,
Giving us heat, light and life.

Sam Loveless (10)
St Benedict's Junior School, Ealing

What Is Blue?

Blue is the pond
As calm as can be.
Blue is a car
As good as new.
Blue is the ocean
Swishing away,
Going to a country far away.
Blue is my wallpaper
Spotty and bright.
Blue is the sky
Calm and light.

Benedict Chippendale (9)
St Benedict's Junior School, Ealing

My Cat Fred

My cat Fred is a fluffy ball of fur,
He sits on the chair and likes to purr.
All day long he sleeps and eats,
And is rather partial to sweets.
Occasionally he brings home a mouse,
My mum kicks it out of the house.

My cat Fred is very sad,
He broke Mum's jug which was very bad.
He ran upstairs in case he got caught,
I could not shout, he's only short.
He danced with my ted,
And wet the bed.

My cat Fred is a very, very bad cat!

Patricia Tran (9)
St Charles RC Primary School, London

Sweets!

Sweets are nice to eat
As a yummy treat
You can crunch them small
Or make them into a ball
You can blow them really big
Then pop them with a twig
I really love sweets.

Chioma Okeke-Aru (8)
St Charles RC Primary School, London

A Poem That Compares Thoughts And Feelings

A person of lies and not of truth
Is like someone who should be stuck in a booth
A friend who comforts you when you're sad
Is like the person who resembles your dad
Someone who gossips behind your back
Is a very uncontrollable maniac
Someone who helps you to find lost things
Is someone who's got control of their things
The person who calls when you think you've no friends
Is a wonderful dream that doesn't have to end . . .

Dean-Emmanuelly Kamna (11)
St Charles RC Primary School, London

Aliens

Are there such things as aliens?
I wonder when I'm in bed at night.
Are they big? Are they small?
Do they hide in our school?
Do they want to steal our teacher?
Maybe they even want to eat her!

Jowayne James (8)
St Charles RC Primary School, London

Space

Jupiter is close to Mars,
With asteroids the size of metal bars,
With Saturn, Neptune and others too,
And the starry sky is navy blue,
With shiny rockets up very high,
Like a giant moon that fills the sky.

Rianna Hinds (9)
St Charles RC Primary School, London

Comparisons

A person of lies and not of truth
Is like someone with a missing tooth
A friend who comforts you when you're sad
Is like your very own dad
Someone who gossips behind your back
Is like an uncontrollable maniac
Someone who helps you find lost things
Is like the master of the rings
The person who calls you when you think you've no friends
Is like a lifetime that never ends.

Simone Almario (10)
St Charles RC Primary School, London

The Mouse

In the early hours of the morning when the sun has not yet risen,
you will hear a sort of snuffling coming from the kitchen door
and out will creep a mouse, aware and alert.
It creeps along the floor, desperately scanning for the leftovers
from dinner.
The mouse scurries along the table and then sniffs about for any small
crumbs just thrown on the floor.
He finds some crumbs, then back to the shadows
of the big kitchen door . . .

Rosie Lim (10)
St James Independent School, London

Who Am I?

I am everywhere that you know
I may be any shape.
I live everywhere.
I am all colours that you can think of.
I make people happy and . . .
What am ?

Aylin Ozbicer (10)
St James Independent School, London

Loneliness Is . . .

Loneliness is a faraway island without any other islands around.
Loneliness is a sad private person or thing that is always
in the corner.
Loneliness is a way of life that nobody wants to be involved in.
Loneliness is a form of suffering, misery and grief.
Loneliness is someone who can be clever but has never heard
of the words 'unity' or 'sharing'.
Loneliness is a little insect all alone on a big anthill.
Loneliness can bring unhappy misery when everybody else
is happy and joyful.
Loneliness is a word that means 'excluded' or 'isolated'.
Loneliness can be like a disease that can get to your heart
and can make you feel so ill that you don't want to be seen in public.

Amy Douglas-Morris (10)
St James Independent School, London

The Two Sea Horses

Down in the magnificence of the dark blue sea, lies a sea horse,
His skin, covered in shimmering emerald,
His eyes, sparkling gold.

He gracefully moves around the sea,
His delicate fins fluttering speedily.

Spinning and twirling, he comes along,
To a turquoise sea horse singing a song.

They meet each other and become good friends,
But little do they know, that their lives are going to come to an end!

A net swept by and caught them side by side,
And that was when their lives, their pleasant lives,
Came to a tragic end.

Ava Halvai (11)
St James Independent School, London

The Sea Is A Smashed Crystal

S is for the swirly aqua sea
M is for the misty sea so free
A is for Antarctica with snow and ice
S is for sunset, so beautiful and nice
H is for Heaven that everyone wishes for
E is for exotic, the most amazing thing you saw
D is for diamonds, shining and glistening more and more

C is for cloudy, always waiting
R is for rippling, never hesitating
Y is for you, always in my mind
S is for sunrise, which always looks fresh and kin.
T is for towering iceberg above the ocean wide
A is for the aqua sea always crashing to the side
L is for *life* alone!

Zoe Hewitt (10)
St James Independent School, London

City In The Sky

There is a city,
a city in the sky
Enchanted by the gleaming palace
made of diamond stars,
abandoned in a shimmer of smashed crystals,
the power,
the passion,
and the gentle lapping of the sun's tide
on the beach of clouds.
The roller coaster ride on a glistening shooting star
and sleeping on a bed floating in the Milky Way.

Imogen Willis (11)
St James Independent School, London

The Free Things In Life Are Best

The free things in life are best
like the river shimmering
and the sunset glimmering.

Or a firework show, *bang!*
Even clashing cymbals, *clang!*

Or when the birds fly
in the aqua-blue sky.

And when it's your birthday
and people say, *'Hip hip hooray!'*

The things that make you feel unstressed
are the free things in life
which are best.

Tara Saheli Vyas (10)
St James Independent School, London

The Wolf

A wolf sits on a cliff, alone
He looks at the surrounding forest
But he is alone
There is a gentle rustle in the bushes
He is not alone!
The cub sees his mother's coat
Dappled with moonlight
But she has come back alone
Soon the mother leaves to hunt
The cub is left alone
A shot from a pistol through the air
He hears his mother's howl . . .
Now he is truly alone.

Ashleigh John (11)
St James Independent School, London

Bubbles!

Imagine bubbles floating over a river,
Sparkling, glimmering, shimmering,

They go through a dappled sunlit garden,
And under a yellowy green tree
With its branches bowing softly down,

To the bubbles, in the enchanted garden.
One bubble twirls around and bursts.
Then, all the other bubbles float up to the aqua-blue sky
And burst too . . .

The loveliness of these things,
So beautiful and simple has gone,

But the memory of them is still there . . .

This is Heaven!

Jessica Cselko (11)
St James Independent School, London

The Spirit Of The Sea

The sea, sparkling as the sun shines down on it.
The spray twinkling before it falls.
Shimmering and twisting,
The spirit seems to bubble with laughter.

The sea has a song of its own,
A lonely, wild song.
It sings it again and again,
The spirit surging, soaring, flying free.

The sea has a melody.
A melody of happiness and laughter.
Surging, gliding,

> *The spirit*
> > *Of the*
> > > *Sea!*

Amanda Ruth Waters (11)
St James Independent School, London

Swimmer

Those three words are important,
`You can see your reflection in the water,
You take caution not to lean over the side too far,
Or you will fall into the aquamarine water.

Those three words are important,
As you wait for those three words,
You think about the electricity running through your body,
You rely on the electricity that gives you energy for speed.

Those three words are important,
You wait and wait for them,
For what seems like hours,
But is only thirty seconds.

Those three words are important,
And if you miss those three words,
You miss everything . . .
Everything!

Those three words are important,
By now you are thinking so hard,
That you can hardly remember them,
You can hear your heart beating in your ears.

Those three words are important . . .

'Ready, steady, go!'

Liberty Ann Pearl (11)
St James Independent School, London

The Flower

F ireworks bursting into bloom
L uminous as droplets of water shining like smashed diamonds
O utstanding multicoloured petals dancing in the breeze
W ater dragons as they circle round the stem
E nchanted smell wafting through the air
R adiant with their small, happy faces smiling up.

Francesca Kynan-Holmes (11)
St James Independent School, London

The Slugslee

Down in the depths of the deep dark sea,
There is an ugly old creature called the Slugslee,
No one has seen it but me and no one I hope will see it.

It moves like a slug when it lumbers about
And never says no to a meal.

He has ten long tentacles all covered in algae,
Which he uses to catch his prey.

Most of the time he sleeps down in the depths
Of what I call hell, but for him it's more like heaven.

He always looks sad for some strange reason
And I think he's good inside,
Something wants to come out of him,
Something good, something fresh, something clean.

I think I might have been dreaming just now
For he is a foul and unpleasant creature.

Down in the depths of the deep dark sea
There is an ugly old creature called the Slugslee.

No one has ever seen it but me and no one I hope will see it.

Tatyana Rutherston (10)
St James Independent School, London

The Beach At Night

The beach at night is an awesome sight, with the fireflies flying away.
When you go into the sea, you will swim with all the little fish.
You will see a magnificent turtle with a shell so beautiful that it looks
like smashed crystal.
He will take you away to the lagoon.
Hooray and *wow!* You have nothing to say.
So when you come to the sea at night, make sure you see it all!

Aarti Nayak (10)
St James Independent School, London

Priceless

It is the diamonds shimmering from its skirt that are dappled
like an enchanted wave.
It was priceless.

It is the gems like fireworks on its coat.
It was priceless.

It is like fireflies in the gentle heat.
It was priceless.

It is the glowing beauty as fresh as Heaven.
It was priceless.

It is the amazing sunset, sleepy and soothing.
It was priceless.

It is the gentle foam lapping over the shattered crystals.
It was priceless.

It is the luminous freedom like the underwater world.
It was priceless.

It is the joyful shimmer like gleaming energy.
It was priceless.

It is the electric power gliding in the misty wind.
It was priceless.

It is the glistening reflection of a wonderful mother.

She *is* priceless!

Olivia Kelly (10)
St James Independent School, London

Loneliness Is . . .

Loneliness is a dark colour all around you.
Loneliness is a swan when a wife or husband has passed away
and is left all alone.
Loneliness is the last piece of broccoli on a plate about to be put
in the bin.
Loneliness is a newborn baby bird being pushed out of the nest
onto the road.
Loneliness is a scuffed, old, beaten tractor in the rain.
Loneliness is one black rose left in the field.
Loneliness is a slow jazz song that no one likes.
Loneliness is a lost child alive in a sandstorm.
Loneliness is one black sock gone pink in the back of Dad's drawer.

Lara Dingemans (10)
St James Independent School, London

'Tis Life

'Tis the future that's beautiful.

'Tis the lifeless, sweet scent of home that is rest.

'Tis the freedom that is silent.

'Tis what we think that drifts away.

'Tis love that's a gift.

'Tis me that's true.

'Tis the time we have but do not use.

That is life!

Elva Vuskovic Enninful (11)
St James Independent School, London

Who Am I?

I'm the one who takes care of unwell and aged people.
I soothe them when they're barking mad about something
they can't express.
I go when it is time but then come back as a jolly sign.
I never die with my enchanting soul.

So the question is . . .

Who am I?

And the answer is . . .

H e a v e n!

Ella Wills (10)
St James Independent School, London

Cake Icing

Oh cake icing, just how enticing.
It looks so good, surely it is the best food.
I wish the glistening stuff could make me healthy or tough,
For then we would have it all the time,
In such flavours as lemon and lime.
Most would adore it and some would deplore it.
But cake icing, oh, cake icing,
I can't get enough of it, even if I were down at the bottom of
a stone-cold pit.

Cake icing is what I would crave for,
It's definitely a delight that's my fave.

Zoë MacLellan (11)
St James Independent School, London

If I Had A Boat

If I had a boat,
I would sail to a faraway land.
Where there's lots of treasure to look at.
It's a wonderful place, it is.
I could dance and dance until I felt sleepy.
I could see all the animals.
It's true, it's true.
There are monkeys, elephants, birds, all sorts.
I love the waves.
They're blue and clear,
Like the wind,
Blowing in your ear.

Elizabeth Witkowski (10)
St James Independent School, London

A Strange Feeling

As my hand brushes against the sand
there is a soft and warm feeling.
My hand goes warm and my body shivers
right down to my toes.
I have never had this feeling before,
the sand on the beach,
the clear view of the shimmering water
and we, all alone!

Nenaz Babaee (11)
St James Independent School, London

Boredom

Boredom is like . . .

Boredom is blank,
it's not bright,
it's just white.

Boredom is like the hands on a clock,
they get slower every time,
they make no noise like a mime.

Boredom is like watching a snail move,
it's so slow,
it will never go.

Boredom is like watching paint dry,
it's never going to dry,
it makes time fly.

That's what boredom is like!

Benedict Parker (9)
St John Evangelist RC Primary School, London

Anger

Anger is like an earthquake in my head.
Anger is like a volcano on my head.
Anger is like a river of lava.
I hate when I am angry.
Anger is like my head popping off my body.
Anger is like a ball hitting my head.

Andrew George Whiting (8)
St John Evangelist RC Primary School, London

Feelings - Anger

It is a feeling that hurts, that no one gets
Like a volcano bursting in my head
It hurts all the time
So I go to my mum
'Mum,' I say
'Pardon, darling,' she says
'Mum, I've got a feeling that you don't get every year
It's like a bursting, exploding volcano
and
   it's
      getting
         on
           my
             nerves!'

Lauren Jade Healy (9)
St John Evangelist RC Primary School, London

Sadness

I am very sad, it feels like no one is there.
Being sad is like the colour black.
I don't like being sad.
Sometimes it makes me mad and a little bit bad.
Sadness is like a crow on my shoulder.
It is like a bird that can't sing in a dull tree.
Being sad is horrible.

Louis Nathan Oliva (8)
St John Evangelist RC Primary School, London

My Best Friend

My best friend Jade is pretty.
A very nice Japanese girl.
Jade is very kind and shares things with me.
She has brown eyes.
She is very good at singing.
She is good at dancing.
She is a very good student at school and at home.
I always play with her every day.
She was born in October, 2001.
She has brown eyes.
She has black hair.
She has brown skin.
She is neat and tidy.
She has two brothers and two sisters.
I never want to leave her.
She never leaves me ever.

Scarlett Malynn (7)
St John Evangelist RC Primary School, London

Anger

Anger is like an erupting volcano, destroying the peace and calm.
Anger tastes like a bowl of hatred and betrayal.
It's like a disease that you have never forgot.
It makes me red with rage.
It makes me upset.
It makes me cry and be mad.
It has many feelings.
It sounds like wood crackling, bricks smashing.
I'm so angry!

Harvey Grace (9)
St John Evangelist RC Primary School, London

My Best Friend

My best friend is called Amanda
She is fun and she has fashion
She plays with me every day
She is very special to me!
You would wish to be her friend
Because she is too kind!
She is in my class
She has a little brother called Cameron
Who is one year old.

Kayleigh Harold (7)
St John Evangelist RC Primary School, London

I Am Love

I love you, you love me,
I look like a red heart to you,
I am as red as a pepper
That you buy in the shop.
Love is like the colour red,
Like an exploding volcano.
Love is like the shape of a heart!
Love is lovely.

Megan Wills (9)
St John Evangelist RC Primary School, London

Fun

Fun is like food.
Fun is like sugar.
Fun is like children playing.
Fun is like a smoothie.
Fun is like playing football.

Alfie Dundon (8)
St John Evangelist RC Primary School, London

Sadness

Sometimes I'm sad, I'm bored and alone,
And sometimes I break my mum's and dad's bed by jumping
in anger.
When the sun shines on me I get very angry
And I feel like throwing a baseball bat at a window because the sun
can blind me.
I'll even hide when I go to the cinema.
I run out because I don't like the film,
And my mum just likes boring films!

Henry Jay White (8)
St John Evangelist RC Primary School, London

Sadness

Sadness is like a night without stars, a sun without heat.
Sadness smells like an old rotten cheese.
Sadness reminds me of the first time I broke up with someone.
Sadness sounds like a friend's footsteps walking away from you,
slowly and sadly.
Sadness looks like a door closing and then the room is silent.
Sadness makes me feel horrible.

Rachel Burgess (8)
St John Evangelist RC Primary School, London

I Am Anger

Anger is red like a fierce exploding volcano.
It sounds like a drum going through my head.
It feels like a big bang going through my brain, *bang, bang, bang!*
I am so angry that I am going to faint.
I am anger, it reminds me of punching a wall!

Tilly Townsend (8)
St John Evangelist RC Primary School, London

Sadness

I feel sad when I am bored,
I feel sad when I am alone,
I feel sad when no one is there beside me,
I feel sad when I have no one to play with,
Being sad is like a rainbow getting duller by the second.
Being sad is like everything around me is grey.
Sadness sounds like thunder in the sky that never stops,
Sadness is like something in your head is about to explode,
Not everything makes me sad but anything without a big smile
will make me sad.

Caighlyn Christina Magee-Biggs (8)
St John Evangelist RC Primary School, London

Sadness

Sadness is like a drip of water from the sky.
Sadness sounds like the wind stopping.
Sadness tastes like slime in a can from a cow.
Sadness feels like a precious thing breaking right in front of you.
Sadness reminds me of a play centre crashing down.
Sadness smells like an old boot in the dirty water.

Andres Florez (8)
St John Evangelist RC Primary School, London

I Am Happy

I am so happy I can laugh like a hyena all day.
I am so happy I can burst with laughter.
I am so happy I can explode like a volcano.
It sounds like an alien in my head pushing me wherever I go!

Andrew Osborne (9)
St John Evangelist RC Primary School, London

Fun, Fun, Fun

Fun is like a summer's morning,
Fun is like sugar,
It smells like sugar,
It looks like two kids playing,
Fun feels like having a snowball fight,
Fun reminds me of my nan.

Connor Gannon (8)
St John Evangelist RC Primary School, London

Happiness

Happiness is yellow like a daffodil's bloom
It feels like a new bed
It tastes like a fresh new seed
It reminds me of the time I used to have
It sounds like something is above
It smells like a potion of love
It looks like you and me
Happiness is the best thing on Earth.

Maeve Johnson (8)
St Mary's RC Primary School, Chiswick

Love

Love is pink like a blossom in the snow,
It reminds me of birds sweeping to and fro.
It smells like perfume made from a rose,
It feels like the sun newly arose.
Love tastes like chocolate sweetly made,
It sounds like romantic music playing in the shade.
Love is a spell never to be broken,
It's a word never to be spoken.

Emer Walsh (8)
St Mary's RC Primary School, Chiswick

Sadness

Sadness is blue like paper being scrunched up.
Sadness is bad like an old dusty house.
It feels like you are being thrown into freezing cold water.
It looks like someone who has no home.
It sounds like drums being banged forever.
It tastes like blood rushing in your mouth.
It reminds me of something that I like dying.
It smells like the dirty sewers being blocked.
Sadness is like a broken heart.

William Edward Walsh (9)
St Mary's RC Primary School, Chiswick

Love

Love is pink like a blossom blooming in a tree.
Love sounds like beautiful music being played.
It reminds me of a ribbon floating in the breeze.
Love smells like sweet-smelling perfume sprayed on someone.
It feels like a soft cushion resting behind my back.
It tastes like a white chocolate heart melting in my mouth.
Love is kisses and hugs being sent to people from people.

Ryan Munasinghe (8)
St Mary's RC Primary School, Chiswick

Hunger

Hunger is peach like an empty stomach.
It looks like a sheet with nothing on it.
It sounds like a painful squeaky noise
And feels like you need food now.
It reminds me of food like chocolate cake
And tastes like nothing at all.
It smells like food everywhere,
But it's really just a breeze blowing my hair.
Hunger is sad knowing there's no food to eat,
But when you do you can have a big feast.

Millie Atherton (8)
St Mary's RC Primary School, Chiswick

Fun

Fun is yellow like a daffodil bursting into bloom.
It tastes like a drop of honey, fresh from the hive.
Fun is laughter, echoing through the park.
It feels like soft feathers falling through the air.
It looks like children playing joyfully in a garden.
It smells like cakes baking in an oven.
It sounds like a golden voice singing down through the clouds.
It reminds me of bouncing on a springy trampoline.

Ciara Clarke (8)
St Mary's RC Primary School, Chiswick

Hunger

Hunger is white like an empty piece of paper
It reminds me of Lent when I fast
It tastes like dirty water scooped up from the ground
It looks like an empty, starving stomach
It smells like a stinky, blocked toilet
It sounds like the disgusting sound of being sick
It feels like jumping out the window
And landing on your head
Hunger is *a huge empty feeling!*

Thomas Rooney (9)
St Mary's RC Primary School, Chiswick

Sadness

Sadness is blue like a puddle of tears.
It tastes like a big gulp of water from the salty sea.
It reminds me of my mum and dad having an argument.
It looks like my worst fear coming out from something.
It feels like a big pain in my stomach that will never get better.
It smells like a bottle of peppers never losing its smell.
It sounds like a loud, noisy baby crying for her bottle.
Sadness is my dream creeping up on me.

Charlotte Purcell (9)
St Mary's RC Primary School, Chiswick

Happiness

Happiness is blue like the fresh, summer sky
It reminds me of the birds flying high
Happiness is a joy beating in your heart
Happiness feels like a plastic covered chart
Happiness looks like a girl in the park
Happiness sounds like a flute passing by
Happiness tastes like an egg ready to fry
Happiness smells like a fresh flower ready to bloom
Happiness is like children running in a room.

Georgina Boyle (9)
St Mary's RC Primary School, Chiswick

Love!

Love is pink like a heart newly made,
It smells like perfume from the company Jade.
It feels like a massage from a pro,
It tastes like a heart-shaped chocolate ready to go.
It sounds like romantic music always going to last,
It reminds me of all the happy times in the past.
Love is a spell never to be broken,
It's a word I have spoken!

Isobel Brophy (9)
St Mary's RC Primary School, Chiswick

Hunger

Hunger is white like a big empty stomach.
It sounds like an empty stomach rumbling.
It feels like a blank sheet of paper.
It reminds me of Jesus in the desert for forty days and forty nights.
It tastes like a very disgusting apple pie.
It looks like a completely empty stomach.
It smells like a big rotten plum pie.
Hunger is like someone dying from lack of food.

Peter Martin-Collar (9)
St Mary's RC Primary School, Chiswick

Sadness

Sadness is grey like a grey sky on a winter day.
It is so sad you can't bear to look at anything or anyone.
It smells like a cold, weary day.
Sadness sounds like a sad conversation in my head.
It tastes like something I would never like to eat.
It reminds me of sad memories.
Sadness is the opposite of happiness
And happiness is something I wish everyone had.

Sarah Duns (9)
St Mary's RC Primary School, Chiswick

Hunger

Hunger is orange like a big hungry tummy.
It smells like an ugly germ trying to escape.
It sounds like a big and scary tornado going round and round.
It feels like an earthquake hurting in my stomach.
It reminds me of Lent when I have to give up tasty food.
It tastes like a bitter lemon in my mouth.
It looks like a fish swimming in the sea.
Hunger is horrible and disgusting.

Chantal O'Toole (9)
St Mary's RC Primary School, Chiswick

Sadness

Sadness is blue like a wet, rainy day.
It reminds me of a grey storm blowing through the forest.
It looks like a puddle of tears on my kitchen floor.
It feels like a waterfall falling down on top of me.
It smells like very salty vinegar on Brussels sprouts.
It sounds like a noisy, loud sound bursting out in my ears.
It tastes like a salty sea waving in the water.
Sadness is like two people breaking up.

Emily Badra (8)
St Mary's RC Primary School, Chiswick

Fun

Fun is green like an everlasting wreath.
It sounds like kids laughing with their friends.
It tastes like chocolate melting in my mouth.
Fun is playing happily with my friends on a very sunny day.
It feels like laying on a very bouncy bed.
It looks like kids playing in the park on a summer's day.
It smells like soft pizza in the oven.
It reminds me of scoring a hat-trick playing football.

Luca James Lota (8)
St Mary's RC Primary School, Chiswick

Happiness

Happiness is yellow like a daffodil swaying in the wind.
It reminds me of a sun shining in the sky.
It feels like a soft petal touching my face.
It sounds like a quiet whistle in your ear.
It tastes like a soft, sugar petal floating in my mouth.
It looks like a beautiful blowing buttercup.
It smells like a strong, sweet smell of pollen.

Eleanor Jones (9)
St Mary's RC Primary School, Chiswick

Fun

Fun is blue like a sky in Heaven.
It feels like a bouncy soft pillow.
It smells like sweet chocolate melting on a hot plate.
It looks like a happy smiling face.
It sounds like joy and happiness coming from everyone in the world.
It tastes like crunchy chocolate in my mouth.
It reminds me of meeting new friends on hot summer days.

Conor Raymie Sugden (9)
St Mary's RC Primary School, Chiswick

Happiness

Happiness is yellow like a daffodil swaying in the wind.
It smells like the beautiful fresh air passing through the town.
It reminds me of the sun shining in the bright blue sky.
It feels like jumping up and down.
It sounds like playing music softly and dancing to it.
It tastes like chocolate melting in your mouth.
It looks like birds making a nest together laughing, singing
And enjoying themselves.
Happiness reminds me of a great day that I enjoyed.

Samantha Fuller (8)
St Mary's RC Primary School, Chiswick

Fun

Fun is green like a glorious opening flower.
Fun is like long fresh grass.
It feels like a soft bag of big pillows.
It looks like a rainbow with so many colours you can't even
                                             think about it.
It smells like fresh perfume of water and flowers.
It sounds like a parade of your favourite instrument.
It tastes like yummy organic chocolate melting in your mouth.
It reminds me of all the glorious times that have happened to me.

Luca Dilieto (8)
St Mary's RC Primary School, Chiswick

Happiness

Happiness is yellow like a flower going and going side to side.
It feels like a soft petal in a breeze.
It sounds like a breeze of the flower flying in the air.
It tastes like a lemon with salt to touch.
It looks like a bowl of sugar.
It smells like blossom in the snow.
It reminds me of snow falling when I was born.

Oliver James Israel (9)
St Mary's RC Primary School, Chiswick

Fun

Fun is orange like a flower growing in a garden.
Fun looks like happiness with all children smiling.
Fun smells like fresh cool air in the bright blue sky.
Fun sounds like joy and happiness that everyone enjoys.
Fun tastes like a pie I am eating freshly from the baker's.
Fun is a flowing cloud in the bright sky with all different colours.
Fun feels like a big fluffy pillow that rests your head at night.
Fun reminds me of a token of my heart that I never forget.

Molly George (8)
St Mary's RC Primary School, Chiswick

Love

Love is pink like a rose blooming.
It tastes like a heart-shaped chocolate melting in my mouth.
It sounds like music echoing through my ears.
It reminds me of a Valentine's cake crunching in my mouth.
It smells like apple pie in the oven.
It feels like a cool sheet.
Love is a heart never to be broken.

John James Edward Dobbs (9)
St Mary's RC Primary School, Chiswick

Fun

Fun is purple like a beautiful flower!
It reminds me of the hot summer.
It looks like a group of children having chocolate.
It smells like lovely lavender.
It sounds like everyone having golden-time.
It feels like melted chocolate cake.

Lydia Hopgood (8)
St Mary's RC Primary School, Chiswick

Happiness

Happiness is yellow like a daffodil blowing in the wind.
It sounds like a bird tweeting to another bird.
It tastes like a juicy, sour lemon which I like to eat.
It looks like a blossom in the snow.
It smells like a good bowl of sugar.
It reminds me of me cuddling a teddy.
It feels like a really soft sofa.
Happiness is the best thing on Earth.

Eoin Murphy (9)
St Mary's RC Primary School, Chiswick

Silence

Silence is white like a blank sheet of paper.
It looks like not a thing is making a sound.
It smells like there is not a thing to eat.
It sounds like an empty plane parked by the runway.
It tastes like nothing is there, not even meat.
It reminds me of a comfy bed sheet wrapped around me.
It feels like not a thing is there, not even someone snoring.
Silence is boring.

Sean Flynn (9)
St Mary's RC Primary School, Chiswick

It's Hard To Find The Right Poem

It was hard to find the right poem
I had loads of ideas,
Like angels and spring
Even my fears.

I could write about
My friends, my family or school,
My pet
And even the swimming pool.

My dreams, my year
My class, my day,
Or going away
On holiday.

My feelings, my future
My cry,
My home, my street
Also my lies.

My imagination
Or something I've written,
I had to choose one
So I chose 'My Little Kitten'.

My Little Kitten

My little kitten
Is a beautiful light brown,
She should be a queen
With a solid gold crown.

She can jump down
And also up,
She is so fit
She won a gold cup.

She is a fast runner
She is trained too,
But she has a little problem
Of going to the loo.

My little kitten
Went out to play
And when she came in
I have to say

She was muddy and dirty
And also mucky,
When my brother saw her
He shouted, 'Yucky.'

So I gave her a bath
But she didn't fight me,
She is a star
And always will be.

Danielle Fearon (9)
St Pauls & All Hallows CE Junior School, Tottenham

The Bully

She does not hit me,
Or physically hurt me,
She leaves no bruises,
That the human eye can see,
But the scars of emotion,
That she leaves behind,
Will remain forever,
Deep inside my soul.
She makes me feel ugly,
Saying no one cares,
I am bleeding on the inside,
Crying on the out.
Beat the bully,
That's what this week is all about.
Together we stand,
Divided we fall,
Beat the bully
And make a better world for us all.

Betty Oppong-Kusi (10)
St Pauls & All Hallows CE Junior School, Tottenham

A Little Thing Called Pain

When you think about what's going on in the world today
Just think about all the pain
Racism is going round and round
Killing people just like it's a lounge
Getting bullied just because of height
So when you go out at night
You won't feel safe
You even might lose an eye
While the killers are marking out some graves
Racism is another problem
Just because of your colour
You could be hurt or bullied
So when you decide to be bad
And join a gang at the age of 13
(Which we don't want to happen)
You might just go round shedding blood
But happily we know that won't happen especially in this school
So when people try to make you do bad things, say what you think
But you know there is a brighter side
That's where we come in
We don't want to throw our lives in the bin
So when we grow up we don't want to be killers, murderers
If you want to be one you'd be a fool
We want to be successful like singers, actors, footballers and more
So if you choose the right path then well done to you
So let's enjoy our freedom while it still lasts.

Ibukun Omibiyi (10)
St Pauls & All Hallows CE Junior School, Tottenham

The Right Way To Deal With A Bully

He knows I'm scared, so he's coming for me,
My hands are clammy, the blood beating around in my head,
I try to move, but my feet are stuck to the ground,
I try to scream, but no sound comes out,
The huge, friendless figure blocks out the sunlight, as he comes
towards me.

He gives a terrible grin that sends a shiver down my spine,
Ms Looby says that if we see bullying, we should tell her,
But we are all so rigid with fear; we don't dare move a muscle,
He tells us if we tell we'll get it hot, before galloping off.

We hold an urgent meeting, some people weeping,
Others cross,
But all agreeing that the bully who made all playtimes rough,
Must be stopped at all costs.

We go and tell Ms Looby, something we've never done before,
Ms Looby sorts it out and he cries and says
He was only trying to get some friends,
He apologises and now we're his friend
And he's as good as good can be,
That's the way to deal with a bully,
Tell the teacher!

Rhoda Akaka (11)
St Pauls & All Hallows CE Junior School, Tottenham

More Than One

More than one thing to write about
More than one
Maybe I could write about
Something that's fun
Or maybe I could write about
A game where you can scream and shout
And clap and dance, run in and out.
There's more than one.
Maybe I could write about
My favourite thing
Or maybe I could write about
A song to sing.
Or maybe I'd write something bad
And something that's extremely sad
Which at the end makes you so glad
There's more than one.
Maybe I could write about
Some animals
Or maybe I could write about
Something that's tall
Or maybe I'd write what I'd done
Today (which was rather fun
Better than adding 2 and 1)
There's more than one.
Maybe I could write about
My class at school
Or maybe I could write about
The swimming pool
There is too much, I just cannot
Put one thing down on what I've got
(I mean paper, not a cot)
Because there's more than one.

Shakira Dyer (10)
St Pauls & All Hallows CE Junior School, Tottenham

Colours

Pink like my cat's paws
slapping and biting the string
with his small pink paw

Green like small, prickly grass
blades of grass tickle my feet
and sway side to side

Brown like hot chocolate
slowly going down my throat
making me very warm

Orange like the sun
slowly starting to burn me
leaving a red mark

Red like the sunset
slowly, slowly going down
making me sleepy

Blue like the nice sea
nice to go in it to swim
always crystal clear

Black like some shadows
always creeping up on me
some are small, some big.

Christina Spanias (9)
St Paul's RC Primary School, Wood Green

Seasons

Winter!
It is a white winter's afternoon.
The air is cold
and a draught coming in.
My friend is cold
and we are shivering.
We wrap up warm.

Spring!
I plant flowers so they will bloom,
pink, bright, blooming blossoms.
Carnations are growing too,
it looks like pretty roses.

Summer!
I wake up in the morning
and it is summer.
I go to the beach
and there is sand on my feet.
I am hot and sweaty,
I splash and splash
in the cold, glittery waters.

Autumn!
It is the evening
and leaves are falling,
red, yellow and orange.
Is the floor covered in leaves?
It is wet and damp,
I don't want to go out anymore!
The trees are brown with not a single leaf left.
Another season is waiting to come.

Christina Paula Tejada (10)
St Paul's RC Primary School, Wood Green

In The Playground

In the playground,
there were children playing.
In the playground,
there was screaming.
In the playground,
there were children playing football.
In the playground,
there were children skipping.
In the playground,
there were some children fighting.
In the playground,
there were children climbing on the climbing frame.
In the playground,
there were children running around the playground.
In the playground,
there were children chatting.
In the playground,
there were some children dancing.
In the playground,
the teacher was looking for problems.
In the playground,
there were some children throwing a ball.
In the playground,
there were some children thinking about work.
After playtime the children did work.
The children said, 'Argh!'

Janine Timog-Santiago (9)
St Paul's RC Primary School, Wood Green

Blue

Blue, blue,
Blue, blue,
As blue as water in the ocean,
As blue as my summer T-shirt.

Blue, blue,
Blue, blue,
As blue as my gloves,
As blue as my shoes can be,
Blue as my football.

Blue, blue,
Blue, blue,
As blue as my ink cartridges,
As blue as a soft baby's blanket,
Blue as can be.

Blue, blue,
Blue, blue,
As blue as our chairs,
As blue as our trays.

As blue as can be . . .

Matthew Tadesse (9)
St Paul's RC Primary School, Wood Green

My Mum

I love my mum, she is the best.
She takes me shopping and sometimes to her work.
Mum lets me sleep after 8 o'clock but only sometimes.
My mum is the best cook, she makes yummy food.
Mum is pretty and very nice.

Marek Dydo (9)
St Paul's RC Primary School, Wood Green

Treats

Chocolate . . .
runny,
melts on my tongue,
for me it's dangerous.

Haribo . . .
sticky,
nice,
the rings
I love.

Ice cream . . .
divine,
juicy, with sprinkles,
luscious,
cooling at times.

Pie . . .
hot, crispy
small or big,
I like all sizes.

Jermayne John (10)
St Paul's RC Primary School, Wood Green

Flowers

See them blowing in the wind
Red, yellow and pink
Hear them swing.

Sweet-scented flowers
Strawberry, sugar and honey.

Everybody loves them
Especially in the summer,
Autumn and spring.

Greyd Monteiro (11)
St Paul's RC Primary School, Wood Green

Save The World!

It's always wet and cold in England,
but it's also hot and sunny in Greece,
but we still never have peace.
Why?

All those black, dark and dirty car fumes,
goes on like a silent killer and harms the atmosphere,
it's always TVs, radios and standby machines!

All that water down the drain,
going to those dark, green, stinking sewers,
also filled with rubbish like
wrappers, cans and dirty boxes,
all that goes to the ocean,
Tol those poor fish!

So people, try and save this planet,
bring it back to when the trees were bright green
and the yellow, pink and blue flowers blossomed at the right time.

Anything can happen,
so act before something nasty comes.
Something bad . . .

Zeeshan Ali Palacios (10)
St Paul's RC Primary School, Wood Green

Cats

I love cats with slimy tongues.
I love cats with their innocent cry.
I love cats with floppy ears.

I love cats when they are chased by dogs.
Cats have dangerous sharp nails.
I love cats when they miaow, miaow.

I love cats with their evil eyes.
Cats are really fast sprinters
And most of all I love cats, *cats!*

Joshua Rodrigues (9)
St Paul's RC Primary School, Wood Green

Christmas Day

It's a cold winter's day,
The music begins to play,
It's Christmas Day!

I run out of Sleeping Beauty's castle
And down the wooden staircase
Into my palace where my presents await.

There right in front of me stands a big tree,
On top of this tree sleeps an angel never to wake.
It was a magical tree with lights and bows of glee,
It really gobsmacked me.

I couldn't believe my eyes, how time flies.
When they said it was Christmas
I thought it was lies.

When I step into winter wonderland I'm amazed.
In the sky I see a red carriage with reindeer,
Exactly like the ones in my dream.
I realised when I opened my eyes it was a surprise.
Right in front of me was Santa Claus
And in his hand was something for me to put under the tree!

Catalina Rose-Calderón (10)
St Paul's RC Primary School, Wood Green

Music

Music oh glorious music,
When I hear music I feel complete!

I dance to the rhythm,
I sway to the beat, once again I feel complete.

I am relaxed,
But when a song comes, I get caught by the infectious beat!

Music notes I play on the piano,
Music oh glorious music!

Keziah Doudy-Yepmo (10)
St Paul's RC Primary School, Wood Green

Mum

I love my mum,
She helps me up,
She keeps me safe.

I love my mum,
She's always nice,
She makes me happy,
She makes me laugh a lot.

I love my mum
She is the best
She is the greatest
She always helps me with my homework.

I love my mum
She keeps me warm
And buys me clothes that are so warm and very soft
I have so much fun with my mum.

I love my mum
She is a wonderful mum, I enjoy myself when I am with her

I love my mum
She is the best, she is loving
She helps me get much better.
I always help my mum
I love my mum so much.

Mia Frappaolo (10)
St Paul's RC Primary School, Wood Green

Magical Rainbow

R ed like pure blood,
A colourful blanket covers us,
I n the indigo sky flies a magpie,
N aughty colours bursting with fun,
B ut blue takes over with control,
O ver far lies a pot of gold,
W herever it is no one will know.

Kirstene Leonor, Milca Mianda & Shaneish Campbell (11)
St Paul's RC Primary School, Wood Green

Different Colours

Yellow is the colour of
a yolk - like daffodils.

Turquoise is the colour of
a pale blue sky.

Pink is the colour of
a velvet rose.

Red is the colour of
a soft, fierce flower.

Orange is the colour of
a blazing hot sunset.

White is the colour of
the moon wearing a white wedding dress.

Grey is the colour of
the weeping clouds.

Silver is the colour of
a shiny medal.

Gold is the colour of
a shiny glowing sun.

Bronze is the colour of
an old clock.

Green is the colour of
spiky grass.

Blue is the colour of
the sky reflecting the sea.

Purple is the colour of
a groovy flower.

Black is the colour of
a stripy zebra.

Jodie White (10)
St Paul's RC Primary School, Wood Green

Blue

Blue ink running slow,
Blue ink going with the flow.

As blue as the big swimming pool,
Jump in, let's go!

As blue as the turquoise summer sky.

As blue as you beautiful twinkling eyes.

A scrunched blue paper lying on the floor.

A big blue poster hanging on the door.

Winter, a blue coat,
Spring, a blue boat!

A small blue bauble hanging from a tree,
A big blue jumper, worn by me!

As blue as the salty seawater.

As blue as my baby daughter.

Blue when you're feeling sad,
Blue when you're with our dad!

Nadia Viveiros Akhtar (10)
St Paul's RC Primary School, Wood Green

Football Is The Best

Football is great,
Football is fun,
Football is good for everyone,
Football is fun when you score like a gun,
Football is great when you are stuck at the front,
Football is over when the whistle is blown,
The whistle is blown when you have scored a goal,
The crowd celebrate when you score a goal.

Thaddeus Rodrigues (11)
St Paul's RC Primary School, Wood Green

Eagle

If I was an eagle
I would catch a mouse
with my long curved claws.

If I was an eagle
I would taste a mouse
juicy and tasty.

If I was an eagle
I would listen very carefully
to the little mouse.

If I was an eagle
I would gaze at my food
a mouse or a fish.

If I was an eagle
I would breathe the air
when I'm flying.

Jakub Morszczyzna (9)
St Paul's RC Primary School, Wood Green

All Over The Place

Birds tweeting early in the morning
All over the place

Adults teaching, middle of the day
All over the place

Hot chocolate bubbling late afternoon
All over the place

Dogs howling late at night
All over the place

Children are liars - never ever ever!
All over
        All over
    All over the place!

Bronwen Lewis (10)
St Paul's RC Primary School, Wood Green

Green

I love the colour green,
green is full of nature.

Green, green,
as green as a colouring pencil,
which draws the nature.

As green as an apple, crunchy
and juicy with worms going out.

Green, green,
as green as blinds with the sun,
running away from the room.

As green as plants
with animas feeding on it.

Green, green,
I love the colour green,
green is full of nature.

Olivia Szymczak (9)
St Paul's RC Primary School, Wood Green

An Idea

An idea popped into my head
So narrow
So small
An idea came into my head
Quickly passing
Would I remember it?

An idea wandered into my head
I wish it would stay
All day and every day

An idea flashed into my head
This time I have remembered it
What a good idea it is.

Ilaria Miele (10)
St Paul's RC Primary School, Wood Green

Solar System

In the solar system,
There are nine worlds.
From Mercury to Mars,
Not the Mars bars
And from Jupiter to Pluto,
Which looks like glue though.

Mars,
Which people call the chocolate bar.
It's not that huge
And it's not very far.

If you go to Venus,
It's as bubbly as Guinness.
It's very, very hot,
Like being in a pot.

Jupiter and the great red spot,
You may think it's really hot,
But you may also think that I'm telling a lie,
When I tell you that it's not.

I've only told you three
Because now it's time for tea.

Norma Molla (10)
St Paul's RC Primary School, Wood Green

A View Of A Dog

Alarm barker
Crazy welcomer
Lazy sleeper
Cat catcher
Greedy eater
Brilliant runner
Loud sneaker.

Tamsin Ray (10)
St Paul's RC Primary School, Wood Green

View Of Snakes

Egg hatcher
    Body cruncher
        Venom biter
            Tongue flicker
        Tail lasher
      Rat eater
    Food gobbler
  Poor sighter
Skin shedder
    Body slider
        Neck strangler
           Vicious combater
        Egg layer
           Fantastic swimmer.

Bernadette Fernandes (10)
St Paul's RC Primary School, Wood Green

Who's That

Who's that?
Who's that?
Whose shadow is over there?
I hear doors banging
I hear hands clapping

Who's that?
Who's that?
Whose shadow is over there?
Is it a man?
Is it a woman?
Oh no it's my mother over there.

Jade Sholaja (11)
St Paul's RC Primary School, Wood Green

An Idea

An idea came
into my mind
so misty
so dark
an idea came
like a firefly
like a snake
came to alight
it crawled about
with a wiggle and a jiggle
an idea came
it came to stay
but it ran away
it jumped down my leg
hopped off my shoe
then flew away.

Elliott Gossett (11)
St Paul's RC Primary School, Wood Green

An Idea Came

An idea came
Into my mind
So quick
So weird
An idea came
Like a bullet
It wheeled about
Like someone cart-wheeling
In my head
An idea came
I felt so joyful
I had to tell someone
But it disappeared
Like an Olympic athlete
Running away.

Raphael Clarke (10)
St Paul's RC Primary School, Wood Green

Talking Animals

Has a turkey ever said hello to you?
Has a dog ever knocked on your door?
Has a pigeon ever asked for your name
Or did it ask more?
Has a cat ever driven a car
Or is it too small?
Has a rhino ever threatened you with speech?
Have you seen a duck shopping for shoes in the mall?
Has a zebra ever been in a hairdresser's?
Has a monkey ever mocked you with speech
Or have you seen one?
Has a tiger ever licked its tongue
And said, 'You look yum!'
Has a chipmunk ever sung?
Has a bat ever boasted about its fangs?
Has a fly ever been to school,
Talking to its mate in the hall?
Has a parrot ever told you to go away?
Have these things ever happened at all?

Well . . .

I'm asking you.

Sinead McDonnell (11)
St Paul's RC Primary School, Wood Green

Puppies!

P uppies are cute.
U p and down they bounce around.
P retty and pink,
P layful and jumpy.
I t looks like a cat with a cotton ball when it plays,
E very puppy jumps and plays.
S o if you have a puppy treat it with care.

Elettra Bailey (11)
St Paul's RC Primary School, Wood Green

Colours

The sun is like a huge circular trophy.
Green is the colour of freshly grown grass.

Red is the colour of pure evil and blood.
Turquoise is the colour of the pretty light sky.

White is the colour of the freezing cold snow on a winter's day.
Orange is the blazing hot sunset.

Blue is the colour of the gleaming sea.
Black is the colour of the spooky night.

White is also the colour of a beautiful pearl.
Blue is also the colour of chewy bubblegum.

The colourful rainbow has blue, violet, yellow, green and indigo.

Serge Raymond Nzabandora (9)
St Paul's RC Primary School, Wood Green

Beautiful Butterfly

B utterfly, butterfly
U tterly beautiful
T *utta, tutta* go their wings
T ruly magnificent
E arth truly has a wonderful gift
R ecently been a caterpillar
F lying around after six months
L ovely colourful wings
Y esterday I saw one with spotted wings

Oh butterfly, what a wonderful thing!

Sephora Serafim (11)
St Paul's RC Primary School, Wood Green

Brush Your Teeth!

I have teeth, so I have to keep them clean.
Brush them to make them gleam and beam.
Use mouthwash to make them extra nice,
Brush, you don't want teeth lice!

The toothpaste must be fluoride,
So bacteria can't hide.
Brush twice a day to make teeth shine,
You know how to clean teeth to make them fine!

So remember to brush your teeth!

Zakia Folson (7)
St Stephen's CE Primary School, Shepherds Bush

Cold As Ice!

Snow melts
Frost lingers
To make us all shout
'Shiver me
Shudder me
Shudder me
Shiver me
Timbers!'

Elizabeth Baird Hutchinson (8)
Sir Thomas Abney School

Star Player

Bring him on
So we will cheer
Let him be with us every year
We will cheer
When he's here.

Benedict Willis (8)
Sir Thomas Abney School

My Auntie

I have this auntie
She's kind to me
She gives me stuff
She doesn't need

When she's on her phone
She likes to be alone
But she doesn't mind
If I am with her.

Maysa Chunara (9)
Sir Thomas Abney School

My Life!

I walk to school
With my cousins
And I see a puddle,
I jump over the water,
I jump over the lake,
I jump over the forbidden ocean,
To see something opaque.

Dru Long (8)
Sir Thomas Abney School

Pirate Wish

I am not rude, not mean!
I am helpful and kind
   And I'll shout, 'Shiver me timbers!' all the time.

I am an ordinary girl
You know what I wish for?

I wish I was a pirate girl
My captain - a pirate boy!

I will call myself Meany Fly
And I'll scream, 'Land ahoy!'
   And my boss will call himself Pegleg.

I will have a cabin girl
But he will have a cabin . . . boy!

I will have five people in my crew
   And we'll scream loudly, 'Avast there!'

But you know my horrible captain will be in my crew too!

 'H- ha pieces of eight!
  Ha-ha land ahoy!
   Ha-ha pirate parrot!'

Ilayda Tuncel (9)
Sir Thomas Abney School

Autumn

Autumn
Starts,

Leaves
Go,

Trees
Moan.

Autumn
Starts,

Leaves
Die,

Oh
My.

Autumn
Starts,

Leaves
Try,
Why sigh?

Nicolas Giraldo (9)
Sir Thomas Abney School

When I Walk To School

When I walk to school
I climb over the wall

When I walk to school
I jump over the garbage bin

When I walk to school
I fly over clouds

When I walk to school
I jump over the bench

When I walk to school
I jump over the wall

When I walk to school
I jump over the moon

When I walk to school
I fly over Saturn

When I walk to school
I fly over the sun

When I walk to school
I jump to Barbados

When I walk to school
I jump over Mars

When I walk to school
I jump over the television

When I walk to school
I hop over Somerset

When I walk to school
I jump over the . . . school!

Charlie Parker (9)
Sir Thomas Abney School

Sky-Blue

The sky is blue, it's so bright
Everybody says come when it's light

The sky is brown, it's so dark
All the birds go to sleep
They sing lovely songs to each other

Dogs and cats are so cold
They have to go home.

Shicera William (8)
Sir Thomas Abney School

The Magic Box

(Based on 'Magic Box' by Kit Wright)

I will put in my box . . .
The feeling of my mum cuddling me

I will put in the box . . .
The taste of salty hot chips

I will put in the box . . .
The teddy bear that my dad gave me when I was 3
It is brown and furry and makes me feel safe

My box is fashioned from
Diamonds, gold and butterfly wings.

Charlie Hendry (9)
Southfield Primary School

Dancing In The Sky

Maybe one day I will find my destiny,
Maybe one day I will take to flight,
Maybe one day I will touch the sky,
Maybe one day, maybe one day.

Want to be on a cloud,
Want to shout out loud,
Hey look at me, I'm dancing in the sky!

I'm not just an ordinary girl,
I'm someone special in the world,
Hey look at me, I'm dancing in the sky.

Maybe one day I will find my destiny,
Maybe one day I will take to flight,
Maybe one day I will touch the sky,
Maybe one day, maybe one day.

Bobby Kakouris (10)
Southfield Primary School

The Magic Box

(Based on 'Magic Box' by Kit Wright)

I will put in the box . . .
A silk top as soft as warm desert sand.

I will put in the box . . .
Juicy and tasty raspberries eaten on a summer's day.

I will put in the box . . .
A golden starry bracelet from my grandparents.

My box is fashioned from silver and gold
With a glittery lid and songs in the corner.

Silvia Piscitelli (10)
Southfield Primary School

The Irreplaceable Mum

If you were a tree without any leaves,
If you were a pan without a handle,
If you were an author without any stories,
I'd still love you, I wouldn't mind that.

If you were a bee without any sting,
If you were a ruler without any numbers,
If you were a car without an engine,
I'd still love you, I wouldn't mind that.

If you were the sun without any light,
If you were a bike without any wheels,
If you were a kite without any wind,
I'd still love you, I wouldn't mind that.

Gustavo Pasqua (8)
Southfield Primary School

The Magic Box

(Based on 'Magic Box' by Kit Wright)

I will put in the box . . .
The softness of my kitten's tummy

I will put in the box . . .
The taste of chocolate melting in my mouth.

I will put in the box . . .
A small brown teddy who used to be my grandpa's
who passed away.

My box is fashioned from
A horse's mane that is knitted.

Milka Goitom (9)
Southfield Primary School

I Would Be Bigger Than You

If a tiger was my puss,
I would be bigger than you.

If the Earth was my ball,
I would be bigger than you.

If a mountain was a molehill,
I would be bigger than you.

If a giant was my dolly,
I would be bigger than you.

If the ocean was a puddle,
I would be bigger than you.

If a skyscraper was my doll's house,
I would be bigger than you.

If Australia was my garden,
I would be bigger than you.

If the sun was my light bulb,
I would be bigger than you.

If the sky was my ceiling,
I would be bigger than you.

But I'm not.

Megan Stevens (9)
Southfield Primary School

Eating - Haiku

Now fish eat snowflakes
Diplodocus eats green trees
Moths always chew vests.

Owen Fullerton (9)
Southfield Primary School

One Family

Silent, swooping, soaring
Over land and sea
Waiting, watching, wishing
Resting in a tree
That is the eagle

Playful, panting, pleasing
Small and sweet when young
Funny, floppy, fabulous
Big, wet, sloppy tongue
That is the dog

Racing, roaring, ravenous
Golden, flowing mane
Mighty, militant, majestic
Very, very vain
That is the lion

Leading, leaping, laughing
Elegantly fun
Terrific, tender, tactical
Playing in the sun
That is the dolphin

Silent, panting, ravenous
United as one
Mighty, watching, laughing
Never, ever gone.

They are the animals!

Eve Chalmers (10)
Southfield Primary School

The Bee

On a hazy summer's day,
When the winter wind is at bay,
I sit and relax but I don't see
The big, fat, hairy bumblebee.

It swoops in through the door
And walks on the ceiling like it was the floor.
A cold summer's breeze rushes in
I close the door, I shouldn't have done it!

After a while the bee wants to get out
So it starts fluttering about.
It flies towards the window like it wasn't there
Then crashes into it in mid-air.

It starts buzzing really loud
And suddenly I wish I wasn't around.
It smashes into the glass trying to escape
If it carries on it'll be bee pancake.

Then it starts being really annoying
Its noise is worse that my dad snoring!
My mum says, 'We need to get rid of the bee,'
And all at once the bee is free!

Lily Johnston (9)
Southfield Primary School

Freedom

F eeling like there is no time at all
R unning, laughing over blood-red poppy fields
E verything is silent except for a distant rumbling but that
　　　　　　　　　doesn't matter because I am alone
D reaming with the lush poppy petals tickling my ear; whispering
O ccasionally I look back but there is nothing but space
M y own world, just mine.

Fabienne Marshall (9)
Southfield Primary School

My Dad

My name is Tallulah and I am eight
I think my dad is really great
I don't know how he copes with my mother
Not to mention my little brother.

Sometimes Dad falls asleep watching telly
My brother and I jump on his hairy belly
And then we fight on the sitting room floor
Until the neighbours bang on the door.

Sometimes he goes to the pub with his friends
And he comes home late, drunk again
In the morning he is tired and grumpy
And goes to work looking lumpy.

I think my dad is very funny
He gives me all my pocket money
So now I'm off to the shops
And this is where my poem stops.

Tallulah Deamer-Warrington (9)
Southfield Primary School

Death Valley

Does anybody live in Death Valley?
Or do the mountains hold
The bones of a millennium
Or the ghost of a story long retold?
Are the hills the stairs to Heaven
Or the rivers the ferries to Hell?
Are the echoes of the ages
An everlasting knell?

Eleanor Booth (11)
The Village School

Where Is The Glory Now?

Snow lay delicately in no-man's-land,
Unprepared to be trodden on
By throbbing feet
And tattered boots.
Soldiers crouched silently,
Thoughts embracing their loved ones.
Nerves sweated through their lice-infested clothes,
In spite of the cold frost of dawn.

We wait for the whistle,
A signal to go over the top.
My hands trembled with fear,
Tension trickled down my spine,
My breath frozen in prayer.

The whistle pierced the silence.
'Go! Go! Go!' officers whispered.
We ran out, terrified,
Guns slouched over our shoulders.

I shot a German.
The innocent look on his face turned to terror as I aimed.
A boy only about sixteen.

Sharing my dug-out with rats,
I sit, squashed, cross-legged,
Smoking carelessly.
A shape appears through the smoke rings,
I picture his face and scream.
Where is the glory now?

Ariella Carolin Mordo (10)
The Village School

The Shadows

The sun cowers like a defeated warrior,
As it melts into the growing shadows.
They swoop and twist,
Laughing disdainfully at everything,
As they linger between the shivering trees.
The shadows weave around gnarled, wizened logs,
Caressing the wrinkled leaves, carelessly.

Dark as the merciless night,
They contort their distorted bodies,
And float,
Elongated,
In the hushing breeze,
Silent as the unmoving stars,
Gentle as rippling water.
The moon shyly peers out from a dusty cloud,
To spy on the shadows that dwell beneath her.

The sun, a bleary, unblinking eye, awakens,
Causing the shadows to fade away.
Slowly,
Silently,
The dark cloak that once engulfed the sky,
Petulantly unfolds,
Revealing a glimpse of blue, free from its cage.
The shadows are nowhere to be seen.
But they will return.

Eliana Benaim (11)
The Village School

Rain From My Window

Lazily, I tumble out of bed,
Still pondering my dramatic dreams.
I draw back my curtains
And peer out of my window.

The dreary, dripping raindrops creep,
Slowly, silently.
Trickling down the glass-like tears on porcelain skin.
The patterns they make,
Sparkle and shimmer in the sunlight.
The window seems to shiver from the cold.
I turn around,
But spin back to see who has won the slow race.

The grumpy clouds turn a wrathful grey,
But one melancholy cloud seems to be weeping,
Dabbing its tears away.
The mischievous puddles twinkle
As if they are winking,
Fragments of rubbish are scattered around
By the wind, above the puddles,
As if they are ice skaters.
I giggle and get ready for school.

Ella Alexander (11)
The Village School

The Blowing Wind

Dancing among frozen bodies,
Elbowing past their delicate figures,
Laughing in their faces.
Its icy breath brushes against your cheek.
It scutters among dark shadows,
It echoes past your ears.
It runs like a valley and weaves between your feet.

The wind swirls around the trees,
Like a whirlpool.
It stings like a swarm of bees.
It sweeps the rusty leaves off the dusty ground
And pulls them up as if they were puppets in a show.
The wind gently strolls between the swaying leaves
And then vanishes.

It rushes through time
In a blink of an eye.
As it floats away it whispers in your ears.
Goodnight. Goodbye.

Georgia Myerson (11)
The Village School

Catching Forty Winks

('If any question why we died
Tell them because our fathers lied' - Rudyard Kipling)

Guns fire,
Bombs explode.
These sounds echoing in our ears,
Edging towards our hearts.

Rats slithering up our backs,
Disease wrapping round our innocent bodies.
Lice tearing our tattered clothes,
Devouring the flesh within.

Catching forty winks when we can,
Dozing off in filthy dug-outs, mud beds.
Sludge oozing over us,
Dragging us into its depths.

A young 'un is ordered to peer over the top,
To spy on German trenches.
Trembling, he ascends the ladder.
A single bullet - he plummets,
Plunging towards his death.

Not dead, but dying,
His poor helpless body writhing in agony,
His white face crying in pain.
The light in his soul extinguished.

Sophie Leigh (10)
The Village School

The Man In The Moon

As a navy velvet cloak covers the daylight sky,
His face slowly appears in the dark shadows of night.

His piercing eyes, colder than ice;
His smile as pure as snow.

The glistening, silver beams,
Reflect on the mournful landscapes,
Enchanting the dark shadows.

His companions, the blissful, blazing stars,
Neighbours by his side
Guard him from good and evil.

Slowly, tenderly he lowers his fragile eyelids
As the crimson beams of daylight emerge.

He has embraced the Earth,
This was his nightly task
And gazed at blessed infants,
Who dreamt of joy.

'The man in the moon'.

Izabella Harrington (11)
The Village School

Seasons

Autumn is a whispering wind carrying fiery orange leaves.
Autumn is a playful child gathering conkers till her bag is bursting.

Winter is snow crunching below my feet.
Winter is frost dazzling like diamonds in the first rays of sunlight,
Winter is the raindrops trickling down the windowpane,
Like tears on a child's cheek.

Spring is flowers dancing in the breeze.
As they murmur to each other,
'My petals are the finest in the kingdom!'
Spring is the sun burning bright on grass turning each blade
to emerald.

Summer is splashing in the cool blue waves of the sea.
Summer is hearing the sound of a bird singing its merry tune.
Summer is before the seasons start again.

Etti Corby (9)
The Village School

My Paint Box

White is like the crystal ice,
or the glass of a window,
or it could be the snow on a winter's morning
or the frost shattering from a windowpane.
White is the clouds in the sky
or the silk on a spider's web.

Green is the grass in the summer
or the leaves swaying in the breeze
or it could be the lizard camouflaged in amongst the grass
or maybe a lily pad balancing on the water,
or the ivy clinging on the wall for dear life.

Ava Shoshan (9)
The Village School

No-Man's-Land

Deafened by the silence, sweat streaking our foreheads,
Hearts pounding, our lips mouthed hopeful prayers.
The whistle shattered the stillness,
Ordering us into no-man's-land.

Scrambling up the ladders,
Stumbling over the top,
We trudged to our deaths,
Pleading for life in no-man's-land.

Orchestras of deadly weapons,
Fanfares of rifles, machine guns and shells,
Trumpeting mortar bombs,
Playing us into no-man's-land.

Wilfred, tangled in barbed wire, screaming
As it clutches and rips his clothes and flesh.
A Boche's bayonet pierced Edgar's heart.
These innocent souls, sacrificed in no-man's-land.

Rosie Burgering (11)
The Village School

I'm Scared Of . . .

I'm scared of you ghosts
Whooshing in the wind,
Scaring everyone around you!

I'm scared of Frankenstein
With his arms falling off
And stitches in his head.

I'm scared of the werewolves
Howling at the moon
Hurting people when the moon is lit.

Ruth Louis (9)
The Village School

Christmas Eve

Silence? Silence fell,
Piercing my pounding ears.
My frostbitten hands still shook,
Nerves standing out like chords.

Singing seeped into my broken heart,
Sweetening my worried mind like syrup.
Varied voices, high and low, floating in gay carols
In a strange, misunderstood tongue.

Dancing? Dancing snowflakes spun elegantly
To the sweet sounds,
Then died on the mud-caked, blood-baked ground.

Boche? Boche approached,
Gingerly, scared, unarmed
Except for the harmonies they bore . . .
Stille nacht, heilige nacht.

Football? Football - enemies played together that Christmas Eve,
Like children, uncompetitive, laughing
On the moonlit, frostbitten no-man's pitch.

Swaps? Swaps. We exchanged
Cigarettes, photographs and match figures,
Speaking broken English and German the best we could.
Fragments of language forming friendships.

Over? Over was our peace.
I trudged back to my trench
Dreading that, tomorrow, I would once again
Be slaughtering.
Not enemies, this time, but my friends.

Ariane Hughes (10)
The Village School

Early One Morning . . .

Early one morning . . .
Radiant sunbeams scrolled across the urban sky.
No one was awake.
It was a white surprise to all the people in the city;
Fragments of satin snowflakes swirling in the light and icy breeze,
Mute and content,
Bluebells, buttercups and heady smells or roses and candytuft
Sprinkled in snow . . .
As cold as a broken heart.
Dappled sunlight weaving through the elegant trees,
Dancing leaves,
Glistening and gleaming snow.

Early one morning . . .
The crimson sun arose from the rippling water of the lake,
No one was awake.
The morning was clear and silent,
The stars slowly shrinking and hiding in the forgotten sky,
Waiting until nightfall,
To dazzle, like a million polished diamonds.
The dainty dew was shimmering on the edges of the pearly lily pads
And towering reeds . . .
The sky turned a deep aquamarine colour
And the fluffy, white clouds were sailing,
Then the crisp night falls again. . .

Georgina Campbell (11)
The Village School

The Bad Weather

I stepped outside when
Weather's changed . . .

The wind passes secrets
To the trees, they dance with excitement.
When it is angry
It strikes the trees
Snapping them like twigs,
Or it might just be a giant's breath.

The rain is little glass crystals
Falling, then melting.
The spiders embroider it in their web.
The grey sky insults the clouds
So they cry and tap on your window
To let you know how sad they are.

The fog is an angry net
Trapping you in the middle of nowhere.
Mysteries lie behind it.
It creeps ghost-like, haunting houses.
It steals the summer sky.

I stepped outside when
Weather's changed . . .

Melina Pelling (10)
The Village School

Rain

R ain in the
A ir
I t
N ever stops!

Katie Gardner (8)
The Village School

The Kiwi

The kiwi is running.
The kiwi is running home.
The kiwi is running.

The kiwi is hunting.
The kiwi is hunting for food.
The kiwi is hunting.

The kiwi is calling.
The kiwi is calling for his mates.
The kiwi is calling.

The kiwi is eating.
The kiwi is eating to fill his tummy.
The kiwi is eating.

The kiwi is hiding.
The kiwi is hiding from the dog.
The kiwi is hiding.

The kiwi is sleeping.
The kiwi is sleeping as he is tired.
The kiwi is sleeping.

Matilda Moffitt (9)
The Village School

Sounds Like Wind

I can hear you, wind.
I can hear you when you are howling up there.
I can hear you when you are blowing up there.
B   l   o   w.
I can hear you when you are whistling up there.
I can hear you when you are calling up there.
B   l   o   w
B   l   o   w.

Chrysoula Anastassopoulos (9)
The Village School

My Idea Of Colours

Blue is the rain trickling onto trees,
Then dribbling down on the pavement,
Making perfect puddles,
Or my stripy blue pyjamas, like the deep, blue, wavy sea,
Going on and on forever more.
It is the enormous sky, just floating there,
Like a huge blanket above our head,
Protecting us from space,
Or it might be a blueberry sweet, fizzing in my mouth,
Until it vanishes into thin air.

Red is the fire extinguisher spraying the burning fire with water,
Red-hot flames burst up like fireworks in the sky,
Or a volcano erupting, with boiling hot lava
Racing down,
Destroying anything it can.
It is blood oozing out of a wounded soldier's leg.

Saskia Soning (9)
The Village School

Garden

I can hear the bees buzzing in the garden
I can hear the leaves swishing
Swish swoosh

I can hear the flowers sing
I can hear the bees that go

> *bzz*
>> *bzz*
>>> *bzz*
>>>> *bzz*

I can hear the nettles saying 'sting, sting, sting'
I can hear the Venus Flytraps getting ready to bite
I can hear the flowers swaying side to side.

Lily Burgering (9)
The Village School

Sweet Dreams

Little sleepy bags,
Living beneath my eyes at night
Are filled with dreams.
As I shut my eyes,
Little fragments of my experiences . . .
Or a stranger's . . .
Weave together
A delicate dream
Which eventually
Plays in my head like a movie.
Dreams are puzzles
Put together by your mind.
Sometimes dreams are warnings,
Or something you wish to happen.
They can be your conscience
Plunging at you while you sleep,
Dreams are little soft, silk night bags
That possess your mind,
So sleep my friend
And have *sweet dreams*.

Emily Steinhouse (10)
The Village School

The Village School Recipe

Take one hundred kilograms of clever girls.
Then mix them all together.
Spread them in the hall for one minute.
Stir them into their maths class.
Add twelve pencils.
Send them out to cool for a while
Pour in a cup of Shakespeare.
Then pepper it with ten teachers.
Send them home with smiley faces.

Valentine Kim (8)
The Village School

Rainbow

Unicorns galloping,
Their enchanted horns painting a rainbow
High in the sky.
Doves flying,
Their feathery wings swooping the sky,
Carrying delicate jewels.
Both nesting on cotton wool clouds
Filled with contentment.

Rainbow whispering,
'Come join my magical land.'

The sun, an artist, painting the raindrops,
Turning them into jewels.
Amethysts, sapphires, emeralds and rubies
Sprinkled on the rainbow's arch.

The rainbow's bridge bursts with radiant colours
Filling the sky.

Maya Gerber (9)
The Village School

Time To Go Home

The scent of gas sinks into a puddle of death
As the dead arise to the sight of bliss.
The beat of shells still pounds in my head, then . . .
Silence falls.

I pull a photograph from my pocket.
My son's smile shines out to me,
Melting the numbness of fear,
Tears of joy break my heart.

The cool breeze sprints round weary soldiers,
Whispering the news.

It is time to go home.

Nicola Osrin (11)
The Village School

Snow

Snow snatches a patch of ground,
Ground huddles under a blanket of snow.
It creeps onto a window,
It sketches a picture of a snowman,
With carrot nose, prune eyes,
A raisin mouth and coal-black buttons.

Snow is a sugar mouse on a plate of ice.
Slowly, gently it crawls to a frosty door,
Wishing it could huddle up in the warmth of the cosy room.
It then becomes cheeky Jack Frost,
Drawing a snowflake on the windowpane.

Then the sun peeps out from a hill,
Melting the snow into puddles, like little ponds.
The sun's reflection is like golden fish in the ponds.
Snowdrops are the only sign that
Snow was once there.

Ellen Gilmour (10)
The Village School

Sounds Like The Sun

I can hear you sun
I can hear you trickle down your beams of light
You sparkle on a hot day
You make me happy
You are so smiley
You dance in the sky
You're as beautiful as a ball gown
Oh sun, please shine on me.

Georgina Miller (9)
The Village School

Sounds Like Mum

Sounds like Mum
Banging on the door
Sounds so noisy
Go away

Sounds like Mum
Listening to the radio
At midnight
Turn it down

Sounds like Mum
Telling me off
I don't know why

Run!

Honor Munden (9)
The Village School

Imagine

Imagine a nose
As big as a hose.

Imagine peas
Sailing the seas.

Imagine a brick
That looked like a chick.

Imagine a lamb
Covered in jam.

Imagine a pig
Doing a jig.

Imagine a snail
Once it's eaten a whale.

Manon-Sophia Gibbs (8)
The Village School

Sounds

Morning

Bus starting and stopping,
People stamping.
Dad saying, 'Get up now!'
Birds singing,
Lucy getting out of bed.

Evening

Lucy shouting,
Neighbours' baby crying.
Tick-tock, tick-tock.
People stamping,
Bus starting and stopping.

Sophie Scrimgeour (7)
The Village School

Dream

I dreamt I was a drum
Making lots of noise

I dreamt I was a milkshake
Sliding through a straw

I dreamt and dreamt

    Then . . .

        Bang!

I woke up.

Georgia Scaife (9)
The Village School

Space

Little Pluto sings with the stars,
Lulling space into an enchanted sleep.
The black hole yawns like a weary child,
After tales of fairies and magic.
When space is hushed it seems as if
Silvery moon casts a spell of eerie, rock-like stillness.
Space unravels like string into a stream,
Then a river,
Now an ocean of coal-black.
Sun arises, the moon's spell too weak
To douse his light and power,
He overtakes moon and beams,
Beams harder than ever before,
Drenching the planets in gold,
Waking them, beckoning them
To join him in the joyous light!

Katie Edge (9)
The Village School

Young Writers Information

We hope you have enjoyed reading this
book - and that you will continue to enjoy it
in the coming years.

If you like reading and writing poetry drop
us a line, or give us a call, and we'll send
you a free information pack.

Alternatively if you would like to order
further copies of this book or any of our
other titles, then please give us a call or
log onto our website at
www.youngwriters.co.uk

**Young Writers Information
Remus House
Coltsfoot Drive
Peterborough
PE2 9JX**

(01733) 890066